D1208347

Bruce Graham of SOM

Bruce Graham of SOM

RIZZOLI
NEW YORK

© 1989 by Electa, Milano
Elemond Arte
Elemond Editori Associati

First published in 1989 in the United States of America by
RIZZOLI INTERNATIONAL PUBLICATIONS, INC.
300 Park Avenue South, New York, New York 10010

All rights reserved
No part of this book may be reproduced in
any manner whatsoever without permission from
Rizzoli International Publications, Inc.

ISBN 0-8478-1087-9
LC 89-42689

Designer
Marcello Francone

NA
737
S53
G72
1989

ROBERT MANNING
STROZIER LIBRARY

FEB 1 1990

Tallahassee, Florida

Printed and bound in Italy

It would be difficult to say with words or music what I feel I can say best with building. I have always seen my work as an architect as a continuum from the moment of my initiation until today (nor is it unique that I should, as others have done, return to directions which had been explored or even built earlier). There are two concurrent notions, if not principles, that have driven my search. Before any formal educational process, I had been fascinated by the possible manipulation of structure and materials to convey new interpretations and focuses of the life experience. Equally compelling is the force that drives me to think this manipulation could only take place if the stage itself was equally directed and managed. To date, the abortive attempts at stage management are very numerous. The number of players is enormous and, almost always, neither visionary nor supportive of the script. It appears rather that the animal instincts of our society fear the dreams that make up civilization. Nevertheless, the attempt, beginning with my arrival in Chicago and continuing to this day, has encompassed work for partial or total planning of this city and others in such projects as the Chicago World's Fair, King's Cross Station in London and Canary Wharf outside London. These projects have convinced me of the viability and the necessity for architects to recapture the lost field of city building. We must wrench this task from the grasp of the uninspired bureaucracy which now lays claim to it under the cloak of democracy, but who are in fact stalwarts of mediocrity.

Joining SOM and leading the firm into the area of urban design was essential to my work, and has become one of the most rewarding aspects of that involvement. In the process I have had the pleasure of working with leading architects from across this nation as well as some from Europe. The rapidity with which that work unfolded in clear directions and solutions is proof, at least to me, that while we all protect the individual vocabulary of a given architectural adventure (properly so), we can agree upon and delight in unexplainable spatial solutions which make up beautiful cities. Working intensely or fleetingly with Stanley Tigerman, Tom Beeby, Frank Gehry, Charlie Moore, David Chipperfield, Harry Cobb, Bob Stern and Steve Eisenour, as well as with my partners, has been most rewarding. Collaboration curbs the individual ego and generates electric

communication through the manipulation of drawings, models and structures to produce the thing which we all love, architecture.

Structure on the other hand is a more privately held tool whether the structure be wood frames, bearing walls, steel frames or concrete tubes. I have been unusually fortunate to work intimately with engineers throughout my life at SOM. Fazlur Khan and Hal Iyengar, both great engineers, lent their talents freely to the wild meandering of my work. We dug deep into dreams and nightmares and searched for architectural adventures with forms and shapes that cursed us as well as, at times, blessed us. In particular, the concrete tube was the most frustrating because its relentless logic seems to prohibit spatial penetrations. The concrete and steel frames, however, I have perceived as a continuation of a four-dimensional grid that is indigenous to architecture and inherent in man-made spaces.

In the city of Chicago, we have created great landscapes of the middle west of America which are obvious yet complex. The boundaries are only what we choose and are rarely externally imposed. The nature of the palette; frames, curtain walls, infill, floor plates, and the crafting thereof, allows for infinite manipulation. It is there that I return again and again to regain strength and vigor. It is there that near certainty of concept appears.

The Hancock building is but a modulation of the grid. Its brutality is deliberate, but it is that dream of departure from the real world that engenders its gigantic quality and yet brings it back to earth and its master, the human spirit.

I have never seen architecture as entertaiment any more than poetry, music, painting or sculpture, but rather as an adventure into the unknown which can extend the human experience beyond the ordinary needs of survival, sanitation and the other necessities. Architecture is at the outset functional, but that function must extend beyond the mundane to matters of the spirit. Functional buildings are a matter of law and we are good at it; but, if the only role is functionality, then architecture becomes a craft like that of medicine. We cannot explain every spatial move except that they must exist for the poetry to exist, and for that purpose does the artist in us live.

Bruce Graham

Contents

Who is Bruce Graham, Anyway?

Monographs about architects, or, more precisely, monographs about their work, generally let the work stand on its own, without bringing nuances of personality into play. Frankly, under most circumstances it is not really important to establish the nature of an architect's personality, except as it relates to the peculiarities of an individual client or a specific project. Most architects, after all, practice their discipline in isolation, the parameters of which are determined by their unique interpretations of culture, user, geometry, philosophy, aesthetics—the elements that have conventionally had an impact on architectural practice. By this definition, then, the personality of the architect is intrinsic to the solutions at which he arrives in this individualistic pursuit. In the case of Bruce Graham, however, this assumption cannot be made.

When an architect spends the majority of his career interacting with and, to some degree exercising control over, a worldwide professional organization composed of over two thousand people, then an examination of his work must take this into account.

The magnitude of the architecture produced by Skidmore, Owings & Merrill (SOM), both in terms of sheer volume of building and the collective energy expended on the process of building, far exceeds that of any contemporary firm, and certainly is immeasurably greater than any previous synergetic architectural effort. At the moment of this writing, SOM and Bruce Graham are, for all practical purposes, indistinguishable. But who is Bruce Graham, and for that matter, who is SOM, anyway?

In the late 1950s, Sigfried Giedion wrote an adventuresome essay in the international architectural journal *Bauen und Wohnen* in which he described the challenge that SOM seemed to be facing, and the commensurate risk, in attempting to produce quality architecture for corporate American clients. In his essay, Giedion wondered if it was possible to introduce aesthetic values into such capitalistic enterprises, where the client's primary concern was profit. Like most authors, Giedion left the question of whether or not this was an appropriate venture, and whether or not it would ultimately succeed, unanswered. But the issue of the nature of SOM's practice, and the fact that the firm was a force to be reckoned with in the corporate, commercial architectural arena, had been raised.

It was at that point in time that I came to know Bruce Graham, who had just been elevated to general partner status in the Chicago office of SOM. I had been hired as a junior designer by his counterpart, Walter A. Netsch, Jr., to work on the Air Force Academy at Colorado Springs, at the closing moments of construction for that immense military complex. The completion of that project coincided with SOM's move to new headquarters in the Inland Steel building, whose authorship both Netsch and Graham share (not without continuing debate as to the extent of each of their roles, I might add). Graham had just become partner-in-charge, and thus, my boss. My experiences in that early period at SOM with Bruce left an indelible mark. It is safe to say that Bruce Graham never had an ambivalent bone in his body. In fact, he has often been criticized for shooting from the hip. That coincidence in our personalities represents as good a reason as any for the authorship of this introduction to his monograph, and goes a long way toward explaining the occasionally tempestuous quality of our connection at that time. While our relationship was distinctly hierarchical by virtue of our relative seniority, that is the nature of most of Graham's professional relationships. Few, if any, are perceived to be his equal. For decades his working methods were perhaps too deftly characterized as instructing or directing. His mode of communication at times appeared to be unidirectional; possibly he considered it a sign of weakness to engage in dialogue with other architects. This was the way in which he felt it necessary to conduct himself in the increasingly large and powerful SOM organization. As his own power grew within, and later beyond, SOM, he appeared to increase the distance he judged necessary to the establishment and maintenance of his authority. Along with the success he attained, I suspect a commensurate loneliness resulted from this self-imposed isolation. While the mythology perpetuated by the partners at SOM is that theirs is a team operation, there is little doubt that Bruce Graham is the definitive team leader.

Now leadership, like vanity, bears fruit that is sour as well as sweet. The conventional wisdom in corporate America (and as a firm SOM is nothing if not corporate in its inclination as well as its clientele) is that movement up the ladder is expedited by political posturing. Bruce Graham is anything but conventional in this sense. It is more than a little heroic to set moral boundaries and express belief systems as candidly as he has done, particularly when this stance often invites antagonism. He has not been entirely consistent in this propensity; on rare occasions he has backed away from a battle that needed fighting. His self-removal from the debates regarding the controversial 1992 Chicago World's Fair was uncharacteristic—and regrettable. Nonetheless, in this age of architects who market their services and in the process conform to the norms of free capitalistic profit motives, Bruce Graham's heroic conduct has been remarkable. The fact that he has taken this stand while a partner in an aggressively marketing-oriented architectural firm, makes his behavior even more notable.

By utilizing his power to fight against those forces in a large organization generally devoted to unconditionally satisfying clients, Bruce Graham has brought to SOM a morality uncommon in such situations. It can be said that failure is a constituent element of heroism. A client of his refers to Graham as a fallen hero. To the degree that this is so, in that he has had to fight continuously against the homogeneity implicit in the work of a gargantuan firm where everyone is accorded equal status, his efforts have made a considerable difference. His explosive personality is directed not only at colleagues, but (often to the dismay of his partners) at his clients as well. With regard to these highly charged characteristics, it is possible to see parallels with the personality of Frank Lloyd Wright. Graham's frustration at the inertia inherent in corporate life has led him into problems not normally associated with an administrative role in an immense architectural firm.

And so, when all is said and done, Bruce Graham is an architect—an individual fighting against the forces that conspire to make normative that which is not always acceptable from a moral viewpoint—not merely a corporate figure in mammoth practice. Through his continuous struggle he has ennobled, rather than diminished, that tradition in architectural practice that separates it from much of the endeavors of humankind.

Stanley Tigerman

City: Neenah, Wisconsin
Client: Kimberly-Clark
Corporation
Two-story executive offices;
one-story 500 × 150 foot general
offices; cafeteria pavilion;
on-grade parking
Black painted steel; clear glass;
natural local stone

In 1956, architecture in America was awakening from twenty-six years of depression and war. Before then, architects and builders were unaware of any craft but that of temporary buildings. The architectural revolution in Chicago was not socially related, as in Europe, but was rather a search for an architecture that would express the technical man. We were learning both how to build buildings and what kind of society this democracy was becoming. We were learning to fit bricks together and to weld steel. Kimberly-Clark was just such a learning process, not only for myself, but for many of my contemporaries. Integration and collaboration with engineers

was almost a religious ritual, anonymity a moral obligation. Buildings were thought to be the product of the cooperative rather than individual poetic statements.
An original headquarters for the well-known paper company is located on a fifty-acre site on Little Lake Buttes des Mortes. Three buildings make up the complex: the general office building, an executive office building, and a cafeteria. Planning a general office building sufficiently flexible to meet the varying space demands and departmental requirements of Kimberly-Clark resulted in the very large 500 × 150 foot, horizontal one-story structure. This glass-clad building is oriented around two landscaped courtyards that pro-

vide the office interiors with natural light. But for moveable partitions, there are no interior walls in the building and all support functions are housed below the main level. Retaining walls of local stone encompass the complex, and all three buildings are constructed of black exposed structural steel. The two-level executive office building is raised over a visitor parking area and the entrance lobby. The cafeteria, a sixty-foot clear span structure, faces the lake and, like the executive building, is connected by passageway to the main office building.

Bibliography: Architectural Record, February 1957; *Bauen & Wohnen*, April 1957; *Milwaukee Journal*, 18 November 1956.

1. Site plan
2-4. Views of one-story general office
building and two-story executive office
building

3

4

11

5

7

8

**Warren Petroleum
Corporation Headquarters
Office Building**

City: Tulsa, Oklahoma
Client: Warren Petroleum
Corporation
Twelve-story office building;
two story cafeteria building
Aluminum and glass curtain
wall; grey, heat-absorbing glass
sunshades

*Warren Petroleum was an early
adventure into the integration of
environmental system despite the
fact that even with what we
learned from Le Corbusier's
experience, we knew very little
about how to deal with inclement
weather. The exterior sheet of
glass, which absorbs heat and
reradiates it to the exterior, was
intuitive and successful.*

The general and executive head-
quarter offices for the Warren Petroleum Corporation occupy a
twelve-story tower and two-story
cafeteria building near downtown
Tulsa. A terrace of Italian travertine, marble, and granite with areas
for plantings links the office tower
and the two-hundred seat employee
cafeteria. The corporation's need
for a high proportion of flexible
private and semi-private offices
resulted in the tower's typical
108×108 foot office floor with a
central service core of 36×46
feet. Four center bay columns are
contained within the service core
permitting a clear span of thirty-six
feet from center core to outside
wall. The furnishings and interior
design of the executive floor, lobbies, and cafeteria were specially
selected by the architects to be in
keeping with the building's architectural quality. The exterior of the
tower consists of aluminum and
glass with projecting balconies that
employ sunshades of gray heat ab-
sorbing glass. The walls of the
ground floor lobby and the cafeteria are of polished aggregate pre-
cast concrete, aluminum, and glass.

Bibliography: Architectural Forum, June
1960; *Architectural Record,* August 1958;
Bauen & Wohnen, February 1960.

9

10

11. *View from executive office*
12. *Exterior at night*

11

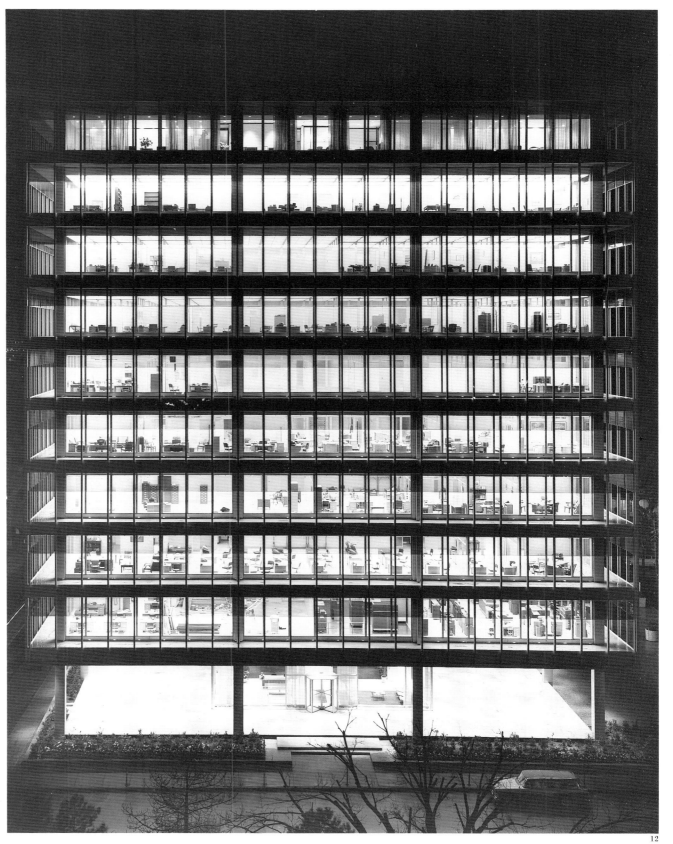

12

15

1958

**Inland Steel Building,
Corporate Headquarters**

*13. Shaft between office tower
and service tower
14. Typical floor plan*

City: Chicago, Illinois
Client: Inland Steel Company
Nineteen-story, sixty-foot clear
space office tower; twenty-five
story service tower
Stainless steel; tinted dual glazing
glass

*The Inland Steel Building was
my first high-rise experience. Still
driven by an innocent view of a
society uncomplicated by
traditions, we were in search of
noble new materials. These
materials had to fit into a city
with a short history. The
traditions of Mies were not as
powerful as the honesty of
structure exhibited by earlier
Chicago architects such as Jenney,
Sullivan, and others. However, the
power of the grid and its hypnotic,
endless quality permeated the
building almost as an extension of
smaller grids found within the
huge American landscape.
Awareness of fine materials began
with this building not only in its
exterior, but also in its*

*furnishings and sculptures.
Structure became even more
religious, and as I look back now,
more poetic.*

This headquarters building was the
first major structure in the Chicago
Loop in more than twenty years.
The building occupies sixty-six percent of its site, and houses the
nineteen-story office tower sepa-
rately from its twenty-five story
service tower in order to provide
interior spaces free from core facilities and columns. A 5 foot
2 inch × 5 foot 2 inch module
governs office partitions and layout. The structural steel framing
includes sixty-foot girders spanning
the office floors and supporting the
beams and steel decking. A stainless
steel curtain wall with tinted, dual

glazing glass encloses the office
tower while stainless steel sheets
provide cladding for columns and
the service tower.

Bibliography: Architectural Forum, May
1955; April 1958; June 1960; Architectural
League of New York, 1960; *Gold Medal
Exhibition of the Building Arts,* 1960; *Archi-
tectural Record,* March 1957; May 1957;
April 1958; *Art in America,* Winter 1957;
Bauen & Wohnen, April 1957; *Chicago
Sun-Times,* 12 September 1982; *Inland Ar-
chitect,* March 1958; *Interiors,* October
1958; January 1959; December 1986; *Pro-
gressive Architecture,* June 1957; *Time,* 10
February 1958.
W. H. Jordy, *American Buildings and Their
Architects,* Anchor Press/Doubleday, Gar-
den City 1976; Museum of Science and
Industry, *A Guide to 150 Years of Chicago
Architecture,* Chicago Review Press, Chica-
go 1985; C. Woodward, *Skidmore, Owings
& Merrill,* Simon and Schuster, New York
1970.

13

14

15. *View of facade looking west*
16. *View across First National Plaza*

Inland Steel

17

18

19

20

21

22

The Upjohn Company, Corporate Headquarters

City: Kalamazoo, Michigan
Client: The Upjohn Company
One and one-half story office building; 432 × 932 foot space frame structure; eight landscaped courtyards
White aluminum; clear glass; natural stone retaining walls

The Upjohn building was an exploration, perhaps following in the footsteps of Gordon Bunshaft, in the design of a total environment, down to the most minute details such as chairs and ashtrays. The building's frame creates spaces that are defined yet endless; they are perfect yet violated so as to contain unexpected experiences such as one might find in a man-made forest. Structure, here, is still the primary articulator of space and the transmitter of ideas.

Set into a gradual incline on a one-hundred acre meadowland site, the one and one-half story headquarters building covers an area of 432 × 432 feet. The building is penetrated by a series of courtyards that feature pools, trees, terraces and sculptures and provide daylight throughout the large structure. The expansive front courtyard is one and one-half stories deep and opens to the building's entrance, while the other, smaller, courtyards are of a one-story depth. The building is covered by a steel space frame structure supported by cross-shaped columns. A continuous 6 × 6 foot modular ceiling of individually-cast plaster coffers set into and expressing the spaceframe, house the building's specially designed, recessed lighting system. The ceiling overhangs the supporting columns, providing a protected walkway around the exterior. An aluminum perimetric frieze of tetrahedrons articulates the roof's exterior edge. The interior open space office is divided by moveable steel and glass partitions that allow flexibility within the modular office system.

23

1 Inner Courts
2 Large two-story inner courts
3 Outdoor Terrace

0 6 12   24

24

Bibliography: Architectural Forum, November 1962; *Architectural Record,* December 1961; *L'Architecture d'Aujourdi'hui,* September 1962; *Arts & Architecture,* May 1962; *Building Progress,* August 1962; *Engineering News-Record,* 19 May 1960; *Inland Architect,* February 1966; *Kalamazoo Gazette,* 22 May 1958; 1 January 1961; 30 July 1961; *Landscape Architecture,* July 1971; *Progressive Architecture,* June 1962.

C. Woodward, *Skidmore, Owings & Merrill.* Simon and Schuster, New York 1970.

25

26

G. W. Roberts

F 7

J. P. Lucus

F 6

27

22

28

29

30

31

32

33

34

35, 36. Inner courtyards

26

37

**United Airlines, Executive
Office Building and Education
and Training Center**

City: Elk Grove Village, Illinois
Client: United Airlines
Two-story office building
Post-stressed 60 × 60 foot
concrete bays framing three
courtyards; setback clear glass
window wall
Education center 44 × 44 foot
concrete bays with flush glass

Since 1962, both the executive office
building and the Education and Training
Center have been expanded.

*United Airlines was an extension
of Upjohn, but executed in
concrete rather than steel, utilizing
large spans. It is a building where
the structure is separated from the
skin, and as an enclosure it
attempts only to borrow a piece of
space to define itself as a very
small part of infinity. The two-
story building stands as a
counterpart to Bunshaft's
Connecticut General building in
its machine-like precision and its
very clear sense of enclosure.
Arbitrariness was not allowed to
disrupt the frame.*

The executive office building is a
two-story structure with basement
and has a 60 × 66 foot bay that
provides flexible interior space. Offices are located on the upper floor
with support facilities on the main
floor. The auditorium, storage, and
executive parking are located in the
basement. The building is organized around three large courts and
four core areas for elevators and
service facilities. A large pond has
been created for storm water reten-
tion at the low point of the site
adjacent to the buildings. The very
large span is achieved by a post-

tensioned reinforced concrete system. The windows are clear glass,
and are set back in aluminum
frames. The concrete structure is
painted white and remains exposed.
The Education and Training Center, is built around a large landscaped court and is similar in ap-
pearance to the executive office
building; it has a forty-four foot
square bay. It contains sleeping and
lounge facilities, staff offices, class-
rooms, and recreational and cafeteria facilities.

Bibliography: Architectural Design, April
1964; *Commerce*, 19 June-7 July 1963.

1 Office
2 Medical
3 Cafeteria
4 Employment
5 Main Entrance

0   25   50   100 ft

38

39

40

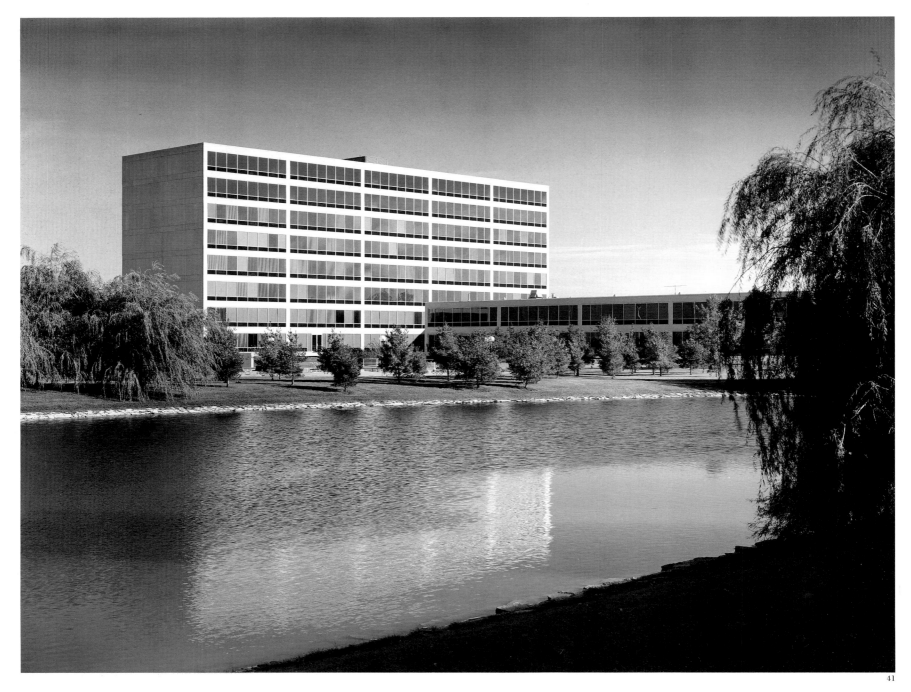

42, 43. Exterior and courtyard of executive office building

42

43

**Business Men's Assurance
Company of America,
Corporate Headquarters**

City: Kansas City, Missouri
Client: Business Men's Assurance
Company of America
Seventeen-story reinforced
concrete tower
Exposed concrete frame; setback
clear glass window wall

*Business Men's Assurance is a
high-rise continuation of the idea
behind United Airlines, but now
in a very delicate steel frame.
Situated at the top of a hill,
around which the wind and birds
travel, the BMA sacrifices
everything for the purity of its
frame and the expression of its
delicacy.*
The BMA Tower is situated on
seven acres and occupies the high-
est elevation in Kansas City. The
nineteen-story office tower rests
on a large raised plaza. Above the
plaza level rise seventeen floors
planned on a 6 × 6 foot module
and devoted to general office use.

The top floor houses executive
office space. The steel framed
structure is clad in white Georgia
marble. The exterior wall of gray
glass placed in black anodized aluminum frames is set back six feet
from the exterior row of columns
providing an open gallery and sun
screen at each floor.

*Bibliography: American Institute of Archi-
tects Journal* (July 1964); *Architectural Forum*, July 1964; *Architectural Record*, October 1972; *Chicago Architectural Journal* 1,
(1981); *Engineering News-Record*, 15 February 1962; *Kansas City Star*, 11 March 1961;
2 July 1961; 12 November 1961; 11 February 1962; 25 October 1962; 20 October
1963; *Kansas City Times*, 15 April 1960; 7
March 1961; 23 November 1961; 10 May
1962; *New York Times*, 14 June 1964.

44. *Detail of exterior*
45. *Typical floor plan*
46. *Exterior view of tower*

44

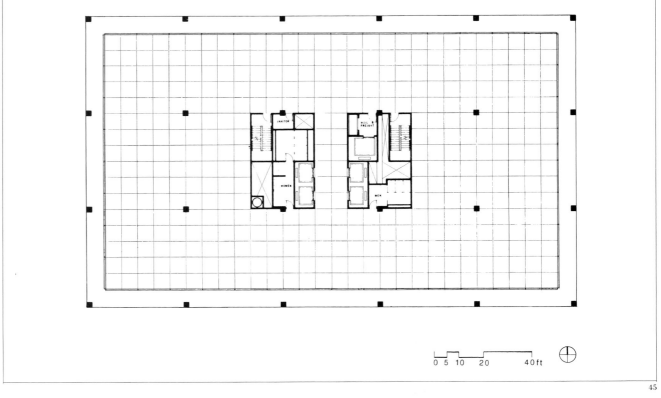

0 5 10   20   40 ft

45

47. Entrance to tower
48. Exterior of tower from east

47

48

49

50

Brunswick Office Building
City: Chicago, Illinois
Client: Washington-Dearborn
Properties, Inc.
Thirty-seven story reinforced
concrete office building with
annex
Exposed painted concrete
structure; tinted glass windows

Richard J. Daley Center
Associate Architects: C.F. Murphy
Associates and Loebl, Schlossman
and Bennett
City: Chicago, Illinois
Client: Chicago Public Building
Commission
Thirty-one story civic building
Exterior clad in Cor-ten steel;
bronze-tinted glass

*The Brunswick Office Building
was instigated by SOM partner
William Hartmann. We searched
for a new kind of structure and
with Faz Khan came up with a
tube structure—the first one of its
type. Originally conceived of as a
steel Cor-ten building, we changed
the Brunswick to a concrete tube
structure so as to reserve that noble
material for the Daley Center
across the street, where a very
large bay was used to express the
dignity of the palace of justice.
That idea was then picked up by
Picasso in the Cor-ten lady which
has become the queen of Chicago.*

Brunswick Office Building

The thirty-seven story Brunswick
office building is located directly
opposite the Richard J. Daley Center (Chicago Civic Center). This
reinforced concrete building is
168×111 feet in plan and em-
ploys a "tube-within-a-tube" structural system that provides much
flexibility in office layout. The
outer tube consists of perimeter
columns placed 9 feet, 4 inches
apart while the inner tube is formed
by the interior core walls. The two
tubes span a distance of thirty-
seven feet. A two-story concrete
girder at the building's base trans-
fers the perimeter columns onto ten
columns that distribute the weight
of the building. As the building rises
in height, a reduction of the column
size and wall thickness decreases
the structural load.

Bibliography: Architectural Forum, April
1966; *Architectural Record*, October 1972;
Chicago Architectural Journal, 1981; *Chica-
go Real Estate Advertiser*, 6 April 1962; 11
September 1964; *Chicago Sun-Times*, 24
August 1962; *Chicago Tribune*, 1 December
1961; *Consulting Engineer*, October 1964;
International Association for Bridge and
Structural Engineering Structures C-23/82,
November 1982; *Kenchiku Bunka*, Novem-
ber 1966 *Progressive Architecture*, August
1966.
C. Woodward, *Skidmore, Owings & Merrill*,
Simon and Schuster, New York 1970.

Richard J. Daley Center

The thirty-one story Daley Center
houses offices and courtrooms for
the Circuit Court of Cook County,
the Supreme Court and the Appel-
late Court of Illinois. The structural bays of this Cor-ten steel building are 87×47 feet.

*Bibliography: American Institute of Archi-
tects Journal*, June 1968; September 1969;
Architectural Design, November 1966; *Architectural Forum*, October 1966; *L'Architecture d'Aujourd'hui*, December 1967-Janu-
ary 1968; *Bauen & Wohnen*, January 1967;
Fortune, December 1966; *Interiors*, April
1966; *Lotus*, 1967-1968; *Progressive Architecture*, October 1966.

51

52

53

54

55

56

55. *North facade seen across Daley Plaza*
from behind the Picasso sculpture
56. *Exterior from northeast*
57. *Interior, executive offices*
58. *Dining room*

57

58

59. Exterior from southeast

60. Daley Center, Daley Plaza and the
Picasso sculpture. Corner of the Brunswick
Building is visible to left

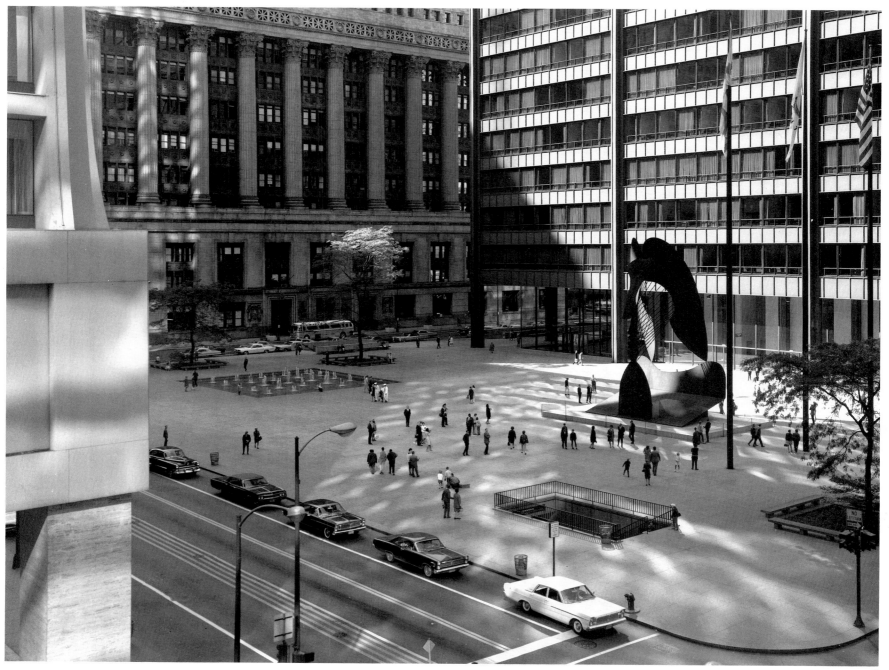

Associate Architects: Yorke Rosenberg Mardall, London
City: Nottingham, England
Client: Boots Pure Drug Company, Ltd.

Exposed one-story steel structure surrounding a sunken courtyard

Bronze anodized aluminum window wall; painted black steel; grey granite

Boots Pure Drug in Nottingham, England was my first experience with building outside of the United States. While it is located in a highly industrial complex, British traditions were kept in mind in designing the frame. The strength of the frame is yet another elaboration of structure, in this case reminiscent of British lofts within which accommodations for a variety of different lifestyles can be effected without violating the definition given by the steel long span frame.

The two-story corporate headquarters is designed around a central, interior courtyard. The main floor is below grade so that the exterior reads as a low-slung, single-story mass. The upper floor surrounds the interior courtyard and provides both individual executive office spaces and an open-plan office area. Key elements of the flexible interior are free-standing carrels with 5 foot, 8 inch partitions and interchangeable parts. The building is enclosed by a bronze anodized aluminum window wall and painted black steel framework. The base is clad in grey granite.

Bibliography: Architectural Record, April 1969; *Architect's Journal,* January 1969; *Building,* 17 January 1969; *Deutsche Bauzeitschrift,* April 1969; *Financial Times,* 6 January 1969.

62

63

64

65

66

67

45

1970

John Hancock Center, Multi-Use Complex

City: Chicago, Illinois
Client: John Hancock Mutual Life Insurance Company

One-hundred story steel structure tower: Floors 1-5 Commercial; 6-12 Parking; 13-41 Office; 44-92 Apartment; 93-100 Television, Observatory, Restaurant, Mechanical

The design of the John Hancock Center, in Chicago, was influenced by its unique site. Just off Lake Shore Drive, it is surrounded by huge, residential high-rise buildings and yet faces one of the city's most attractive commercial streets. John Hancock insisted on producing a tall building with residences above, offices and commercial uses below. The search for a new kind of structure which would accommodate multiple uses and also express the scale and grandeur of a one-hundred-story tower, lead Dr. Khan and me to the diagonal tube. It was as essential to us to expose the structure of this mammoth as it is to perceive the structure of the Eiffel Tower, for in Chicago, honesty of structure has become a tradition.

Situated on prestigious North Michigan Avenue, the one-hundred-story, multi-use tower tapers from bottom to top in order to accommodate the different floor space requirements of a variety of uses. Commercial spaces occupy the base of the tower while parking, office, and residential zones rise above. The tapered form provides structural as well as space efficiency. The exterior columns and spandrel beams, together with the diagonal members and structural floors, create the steel tube. The diagonals, spandrels and columns are clearly articulated to depict the primary elements of this tube. Less than thirty pounds of steel per square foot of floor area were used in the building, equalling that of a forty- to fifty-story traditional tower. The exterior cladding is black anodized aluminum with tinted bronze glass.

68

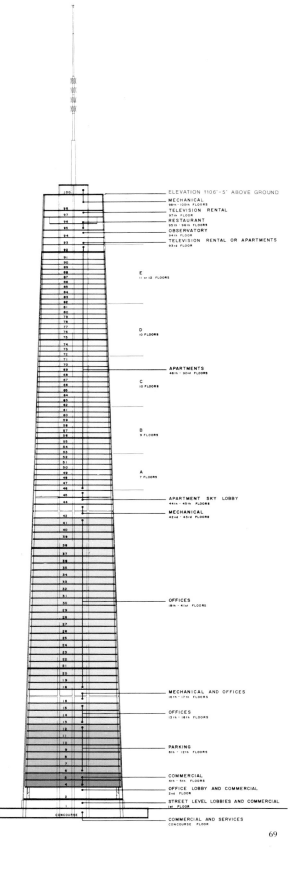

ELEVATION 1106'-5" ABOVE GROUND
MECHANICAL 98th-100th FLOORS
TELEVISION RENTAL 97th FLOOR
RESTAURANT 95th-96th FLOORS
OBSERVATORY 94th FLOOR
TELEVISION RENTAL OR APARTMENTS 93rd FLOOR

E 11 or 12 FLOORS

D 10 FLOORS

APARTMENTS 44th-92nd FLOORS

C 10 FLOORS

B 9 FLOORS

A 7 FLOORS

APARTMENT SKY LOBBY 44th-45th FLOORS
MECHANICAL 42nd-43rd FLOORS

OFFICES 18th-41st FLOORS

MECHANICAL AND OFFICES 16th-17th FLOORS
OFFICES 13th-16th FLOORS

PARKING 6th-12th FLOORS

COMMERCIAL 4th-5th FLOORS
OFFICE LOBBY AND COMMERCIAL 2nd FLOOR
STREET LEVEL LOBBIES AND COMMERCIAL 1st FLOOR

COMMERCIAL AND SERVICES CONCOURSE FLOOR

69

68. *Exterior of the Hancock Center from the Water Tower*
69. *Section*
70. *Skyline of North Michigan Avenue from Lake Michigan*

Bibliography: American Institute of Architects Journal, October 1980; *Architectural Forum*, June 1968; July/August 1970; *Architectural Record*, January 1967; October 1972; *Architectural Review*, April 1972; *Architecture and Urbanism*, January 1974; *Arkitektea*, 1967; *Building Design & Construction*, March 1986; *Business Week*, 2 April 1966; *Chicago Architectural Journal*, 1981; *Chicago Daily News*, 16 August 1967; *Chicago Sun-Times*, 17 September 1972; *Chicago Tribune*, 12 September 1965; 23 January 1966; 3 September 1967; 5 August 1984; 12 October 1986; *Commerce*, April 1965; *Design Book Review*, Fall 1988; *Fortune*, February 1973; *Inland Architect*, July 1966; *Interior Design*, November 1987; *Journal of the American Institute of Architects*, October 1980; *Los Angeles Times*, 31 January 1977; *National Geographic*, vol. 175, no. 2, February 1989; *New York Times*, 8 May 1983; *Perspecta*, 1967; *Real Estate Forum*, November 1969; *Scientific American*, February 1974; *Time*, 2 April 1965.

N.A. Owings, *The American Aesthetic*, Harper & Row, New York 1969.

70

John Hancock Center

71. *Sky lobby on transit floor between offices and apartments*

72. *Exterior looking up from plaza*

71

72

73

74

75

76

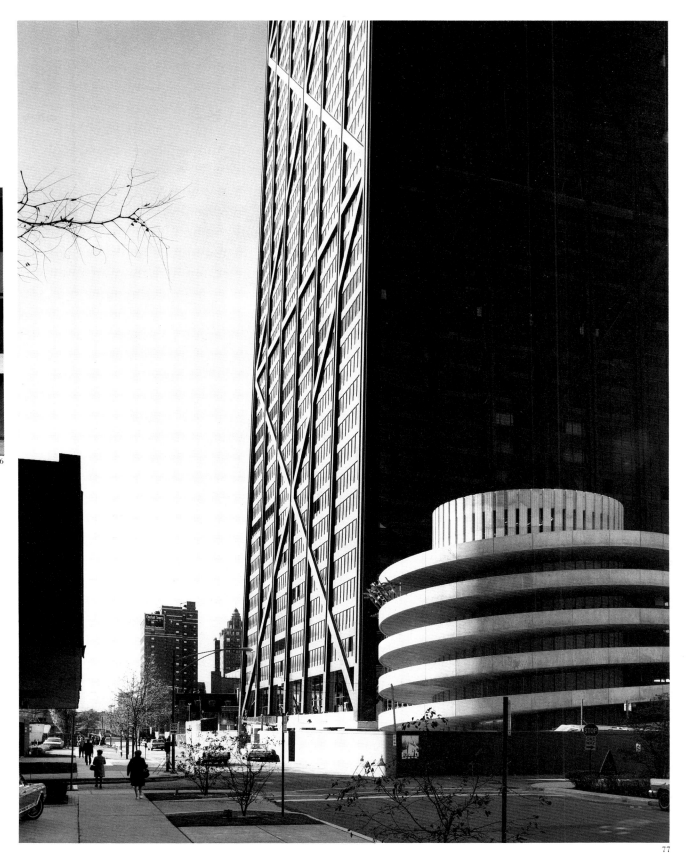

77

City: Houston, Texas
Client: Gerald D. Hines Interests
Fifty-two story office tower
Travertine cladding; bronze-colored glass

One Shell Plaza in Houston occurred when that city was made up of sand-colored buildings and had a sense of urbanism, which it has since lost. The concrete tube, with its forces of gravity clearly articulated on the exterior, served the same purpose as the diagonals of John Hancock; however, the materials were selected to fit in with the green Pin Oaks and sandy Texas travertine.

When completed in 1971, the fifty-two story One Shell Plaza was the tallest lightweight reinforced concrete structure west of the Mississippi River. The building rests on a raised podium and faces City Hall Park. Parking areas and a shopping mall extend beneath the podium as well as a connecting tunnel to the city's existing network of downtown, subsurface shopping arcades. The building's reinforced concrete structural system follows the "tube-within-a-tube" concept with a shear wall core forming the interior tube. The travertine-clad exterior is framed by closely spaced columns which create a load-bearing rectangular tube. The increased depth of columns at eight points, while acting as supplementary wind-bracing, gives the impression of a softly undulating exterior wall. An approximately eight-foot thick concrete "floating" pad supports and distributes the weight of the tower. Windows are glazed with bronze colored glass.

Bibliography: Architectural Design, January 1972; *Architectural Forum,* April 1972; *Architecture and Urbanism,* January 1974; *Fortune,* February 1973; *L'Industria Italiana del Cemento,* May 1974,

D. Guise, *Design and Technology in Architecture,* New York 1985.

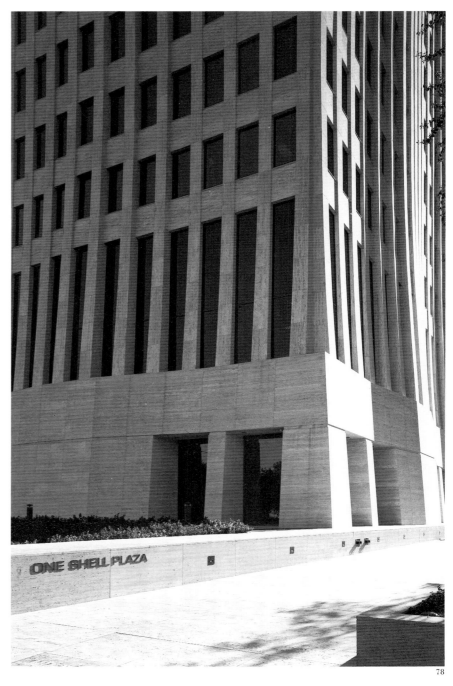

ONE SHELL PLAZA

78

78. *Detail of base*
79. *Mid-rise floor plan and mezzanine floor plan*

79

80

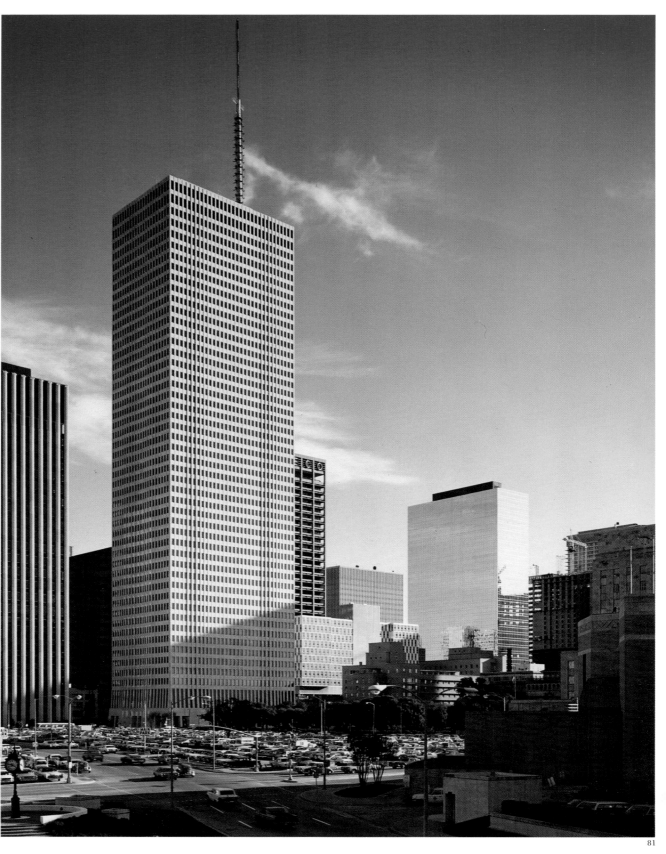

81

80, 81. *Views of exterior*
82. *Detail of base to show wind bracing*

1974, 1985

Sears Tower, Corporate Headquarters and Sears Tower Revitalization Project

City: Chicago, Illinois
Client: Sears, Roebuck and Company
110-story steel structure;
75 × 75 foot clear span bays
Black aluminum window wall; bronze tinted glass

Tall buildings are man-made. Towers have historically been not only the pride of their temporary owners, but of their cities as well. So the Sears Tower, one more mountain, was created for this city on the plains. Sears is very direct in its structural solution, a new concept of cluster tubes, originally fifteen, reduced to nine when the hotel was eliminated from the plan. The Sears Tower itself is much like the idea behind San Gimignano, but unlike most tall buildings in New York, it is a tower of the people, not the palace of a bank.

The Sears Tower is the world's tallest building. The stepback geometry of the 110-story tower was developed in response to the interior space requirements of Sears, Roebuck and Company. The configuration incorporates the unusually large office floors necessary to Sears' operation along with a variety of smaller floors. The building plan consists of nine 75 × 75 foot column-free squares at the base. Floor sizes are then reduced by eliminating 75 × 75 foot increments at varying levels as the tower rises. A system of double-deck express elevators provides effective vertical transportation, carrying passengers to either of two skylobbies where transfer to single local elevators serving individual floors occurs. The tower is clad in black aluminum and bronze-tinted glass. In 1985, the tower lobby and commercial concourse levels were enlarged and reorganized in response to the varied circulation patterns of tourists and workers. Major changes were made to the interior public spaces including a new entrance on Jackson Boulevard and a vaulted, glass-enclosed entrance on Wacker Drive. New commercial areas at ground level were added as well as below-house boutiques, dining facilities and a Chicago-oriented visitor's center.

Bibliography: American Institute of Steel Construction Architectural Awards of Excellence, 1975; *Architect and Builder,* December 1970; *Architectural Forum,* January/February 1974; *Architectural Record,* October 1972; *Architecture Plus,* August 1973; *Building Design,* 20 April 1984; 27 April 1984; *Chicago,* November 1987; *Chicago Architectural Journal,* 1981; *Chicago Sun-Times,* 28 July 1970; 23 August 1970; 31 December 1972; 4 December 1977; 1 February 1984; 30 May 1985; 17 June 1985; *Chicago Tribune,* 28 July 1970; 24 June 1973; 3 February 1974; 31 July 1974; 14 November 1983; 19 February 1984; 17 November 1985; *Civil Engineering-ASCE,* November 1972; *Crain's Chicago Business,* 6 February 1984; 22 April 1985; *Domus,* May 1974; *Engineering News Record,* 26 August 1971; *Forbes,* 1 October 1974; *Form & Function,* 1975; *Fortune;* February 1973; *Historic Preservation,* June 1985; *Inland Architect,* November 1976; May-June 1985; *Interior Design,* December 1974; *Interiors,* February 1975; *International Association for Bridge and Structural Engineering,* November 1982; *New York Times,* 8 April 1984; *Progressive Architecture,* May 1986.

American Iron and Steel Institute, *Contemporary Structures.* Consultant, Vincent Scully, Jr., Washington, D.C.

83

TYPICAL LOWER FLOOR

TYPICAL SKY LOBBY

TYPICAL INTERMEDIATE FLOOR

TYPICAL UPPER FLOOR

0 15 30   60 75ft

84

83. Exterior
84. Typical floor plans at different levels
85. Section showing elevator system
86. View of exterior from the southeast

PENTHOUSE
COOLING TOWERS
MECHANICAL
OBSERVATORY

MECHANICAL

SKY LOBBY
SKY LOBBY
MECHANICAL

SKY LOBBY
SKY LOBBY
MECHANICAL
MECHANICAL

MECHANICAL
MEZZANINE
PLAZA
FRANKLIN CONCOURSE
LOWER LEVEL 1
LOWER LEVEL 2
LOWER LEVEL 3
SHUTTLE
SHUTTLE
OBSERVATORY
FREIGHT

109
103
100
95
90
85
80
75
70
65
60
55
50
45
40
35
30
25
20
15
10
5

85

86

87

88

Sears Tower

87. Tower under construction
88. Aerial view from the southwest
89, 90. Views of tower from south
and north

89

90

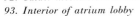

91. *Exterior of atrium lobby addition
looking north up Wacker Drive*
92. *Calder mechanical mobile in lobby*
93. *Interior of atrium lobby*

91

60

92

93

City: Wichita, Kansas
Client: Fourth Financial Bank and Trust Company

Ten-story structure of reinforced concrete pylons with 80 × 80 foot clear span steel decks

Exposed painted concrete and painted steel; bronze

Certain cities demand towers and in other cities such powerful elements should not exist— Wichita, Kansas is such a place. Life in this small mid-western town is at the ground, vistas do not exist. The harshness of the wind and climate demanded the creation of an internal space. The solution was to construct a grand civic plaza inside the building, framed by purely expressed structural elements.

Fourth Financial Center, headquarters of the Fourth National Bank and Trust Company, was an important contribution to central urban renewal in Wichita, Kansas. Perceived as a catalyst for the future development of the community, Fourth Financial was one of the first elements in the planned renewal of the city's Central Business District. Four giant skylights illuminate the nine-story entrance lobby and the 160 square foot interior landscaped courtyard. Interior clear glass walls separate the lobby from banking, office and retail spaces which form a deep L-shape within. Two bronze-tinted street walls provide year-round temperature and solar control. The reinforced concrete pylons rising between eighty-foot spans house the mechanical and electrical systems as well as the firestairs. A glazed pedestrian bridge on the second level connects the building to a downtown walkway system.

Bibliography: American Institute of Architect's Journal, October 1977; American Institute of Steel Construction Architectural Awards of Excellence, 1975; Baumeister, October 1978; Deutsche Bauzeitung, 1980; Space Design, May 1979; Wichita Eagle and Beacon, 15 January 1972; 13 October 1974.

94

95

Fourth Financial Center

96. *View from exterior into lobby showing Calder mobile*
97, 98. *Interiors of lobby*

96

99

100

101

102

First Wisconsin Plaza, Bank and Office Building

City: Madison, Wisconsin
Client: First Wisconsin Development Corporation
Nine-story office building
White painted aluminum mullions; double-glazed clear glass

103

First Wisconsin Plaza in Madison, Wisconsin presented another opportunity to create a large volume of protected space containing a building. Serving as a prototype, it became rather popular and was labeled as an "atrium" building. We, however, were more concerned with the urban relationship of the exterior wall and its ability to define the public square and Wisconsin State Capitol. First Wisconsin Plaza is one of those buildings that is a fragment of what might have been. It was my dream that the entire Capitol Square be circumscribed by a gallery of glass which would serve as a green space in winter, and as a public square in summer. Obviously, energy is saved in this building, and the building is put to the larger purpose of an architectural experience.

This nine-story bank and office building in downtown Madison was the first building constructed in an area designated for redevelopment. The all-glass structure incorporates expansive internal open space and is oriented toward the adjacent Capitol Square and Wisconsin State Capitol building which was designed by George B. Post and completed in 1917.

The back of the building is a straight, nine-story wall of glass, while the front steps down with sloping glass roofs to the first floor. The banking facilities, located on the lower, ground and first levels, penetrate deep into the building, providing generous space for the thirty-foot high atrium. Offices on the upper floors wrap around a fourth floor roof garden on three sides and have unobstructed views of the centrally located Capitol Square. The Wisconsin climate dictated the spacious, airy, internal environment of the building. The use of a high-tech curtain wall eliminated the need for typical spandrel panels and provided an economical solution for the building's skin of white painted aluminum mullions and double-glazed glass in 3×5 foot panels. All structural and mechanical elements are exposed and expressed as design elements. A series of air risers and induction units painted blue and water risers painted yellow are visible and are set behind an outer grid of white mullions. Five murals designed by Valerio Adami integrate the open banking space of the main floor with the bright color scheme of the internal garden areas, while the rather informal quality of the exposed structure is given a sense of grandeur by the clear views of the Wisconsin State Capitol building.

Bibliography: Baumeister, April 1978; *Connaissance des Arts*, April 1977; *Deutsche Bauzeitung*, January 1980; *Interiors*, September 1975.

SITE PLAN

104

103. *View into bank lobby*
104. *Site plan*
105, 106. *Exterior*

105

106

*107. Exterior view of north elevation
and Wisconsin State Capitol*

107

108

1974

**W.D. & H.O. Wills,
Tobacco Processing Plant
and Corporate Headquarters**

109. Detail of Cor-ten structure
110. Site plan

City: Bristol, England
Client: Imperial Tobacco Group,
Ltd.
300 × 700 foot column-free
production space; seven-story
office building
Exposed Cor-ten steel and tinted
glass

*W.D. & H.O. Wills continued
our preoccupation with structure,
but in this case we were
influenced by Isambard Brunel's
grand Clifton Suspension Bridge.
The trusses above the roof of
Wills, therefore, while functional,
were a compliment to the grand
engineering tradition of that
country. Collaboration with YRM
of London was rewarding and
immensely helpful in that it gave
a new perspective both to my work
in the U.S. and to my*
*understanding of the root forces of
our society.*

The Tobacco Processing Plant
and Corporate Headquarters office building for W.D. & H.O. Wills
are located on a gently sloping
fifty-seven acre site. The plant
contains a 300 × 700 foot, column-free production space, thereby providing maximum flexibility
for the processing machinery. The
seven-story office building sits upon a two-story base that houses
support facilities, while the headquarters space occupies the remaining five stories. The buildings
surround an artificial lake located
on the site, and the buildings are all
clad in Cor-ten steel with bronze
windows.

Bibliography: Architect's Journal, 6 May
1987; *Architectural Review,* October 1975;
Building Design, 23 March 1973; *Deutsche
Bauzeitschrift,* July 1977; *Financial Times,*
15 October 1975; 11 November 1976; *Progressive Architecture,* June 1976; *Royal Institute of British Architects Journal,* August
1976; *The Times,* 13 September 1976.

109

0 20 40   80 M

110

111. Aerial view of complex
112. Overall view of plant and surrounding country with Brunel's Clifton Suspension Bridge in distance

111

112

113. Exterior of office and headquarters building

113

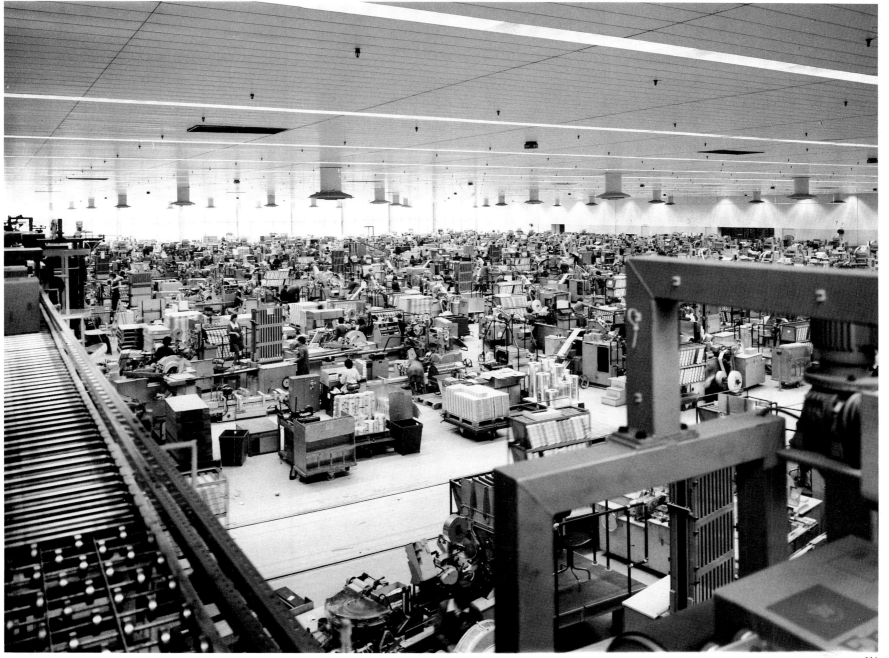

114

Baxter Travenol Laboratories, Inc., Corporate Headquarters

City: Deerfield, Illinois
Client: Baxter Travenol Laboratories, Inc.

One-story central facility building; four general office pavilions; two double-helix stepped-steel garages; entire complex connected by second-level bridges

In the plains of Illinois, the idea behind Baxter Travenol was of buildings that expand as nature expands and a master plan that would be complete at each stage of expansion. The central building was intended as a building, not for management, but for employees as a symbol of their endeavors, and as a place where work would be dignified.
The cable structure for the large roof was not only efficient, but also, by its presence, created a grand space that appears as a very gentle captive of the endless expanse of the Middle West. Detailing, by this time in my life and that of SOM, had reached a degree of sophistication we did not foresee in earlier work. The group of architects and engineers with whom I have had the pleasure of working had become master craftsmen and as such were able to apply high technology where *necessary and simple ideas where appropriate.*

The Corporate Headquarters for Baxter Travenol, Inc. is situated on a rolling 179-acre site northwest of Chicago. A master plan was designed to guide the company's ongoing reorganization and expansion. The complex consists of a central facilities building, four general office pavilions, which flank the north and south sides of the central building, an executive office building, and two double-helix, stepped-steel garages concealed from view by natural plantings. The entire development is linked by an underground pedestrian network and by second-level bridges. The twin masts of the central facilities building stayed-cable, suspended roof not only provide a focus for the site, but also create a local identity. The building's large free span interior houses an auditorium, training center and one-thou- sand-seat, twenty-four-foot high cafeteria. The connecting two- and three-story office pavilions are organized for open-plan work stations and take advantage of daylight and expansive views of the site. These pavilions constitute a flexible cluster of modules that can easily accommodate expansion through the addition of a similar long span steel structure.
The exterior cladding of the buildings is an off-white painted metal with infill panels of full-height, semi-reflective dual glazing set in stainless steel mullions.

Bibliography: American Institute of Steel Construction Architectural Awards of Excellence, 1975; *Architectural Review*, October 1977; *Architettura*, December 1977; *Building Design & Construction*, January 1976; *Deutsche Bauzeitung*, December 1977; *Inland Architect*, November 1976; *International Association for Bridge and Structural Engineering*, November 1982.

115

115, 116. Exterior views
117. Site plan

116

0 100 200   400 ft

117

77

*118-121. Exterior views showing
connecting glazed pedestrian bridges*

118

119

120

121

79

122

122. Interior of glazed pedestrian bridge
123, 124. Pedestrian walkways

123

124

Baxter Travenol

125

126

127

82

125-127. *Interior views showing curved stairs and etched glass screen*
128, 129. *Views of cafeteria*

128

129

**Banco de Occidente, Banco
de Occidente Zone 1 and
Montufar**

City: Guatemala City, Guatemala
Client: Banco de Occidente

*Banco de Occidente in Guatemala
City was done around the same
time as Baxter Travenol. We used
materials particular to Guatemala
and the structure, in this case, was
a bearing wall. The use of native
tiles and natural ventilation
captured the benign climate of
that city. Each building's sense of
enclosure and their public and
private spaces are not in the
tradition of Chicago, but of
Guatemala City.*

The Banco de Occidente headquarters and branch banking facilities were constructed for one of the
oldest banking institutions in Guatemala. The largest of the three,
Zone 1, is the original headquarters
and is located in the center of the
city's oldest section, while the remaining two are suburban branch
banks. Designed to relate to the
surrounding contextual influences
of traditional Guatemalan architecture, each of the three buildings
responds to its unique program and
site constraints. Architectural con-
tinuity is retained in each through
the use of traditional and indigenous colors, textures, materials and
patterns of light and shadow. A
common design was used for banking elements such as the teller
counters, check writing stands,
platform office, work stations and
interior furnishings. Local materials such as stucco, mahogany and
volcanic stone pavers, and local
architectural concepts of open
courtyards, terraces, walled-in gardens, fountains and trellises were
used throughout to reinforce the
relationship of these buildings to
their Guatemalan context. Furniture and fabrics designed by SOM
were manufactured in Guatemala
City for use in the bank buildings.

130

130. Exterior
131. Section and ground floor plan

Banco de Occidente Zone 1

The headquarters office consists of public facilities at level one, executive offices and semi-public facilities at level two, and employee and non-public uses on level three. The building is designed around an interior/exterior courtyard which is covered with a translucent fabric roof that allows soft light to enter, but also reduces the impact of solar heat. A clear spatial relationship exists between the courtyard space, the two-story banking hall, the office functions and the exterior terrace on the third floor. Terrace and setback openings control light while wood louvers modulate ventilation. The exterior consists primarily of textured stucco, and a stone base provides a durable surface for this highly frequented area.

Montufar

This eight-teller branch bank is completely surrounded by party walls, and entrances occur at two points within an existing shopping center. Natural light and ventilation enter the bank through skylights. A spacious sky lit courtyard and a reflecting pool enliven and lend a sense of openness to the small bank.

Bibliography: American Institute of Architects Journal, Mid-May 1981, AIA Honor Awards; *Architectural Record,* May 1981; August 1981; *Chicago Tribune,* 21 June 1981; *Proq. Arquitectura Piseno Urbanismo Industrias,* April 1984; *Space Design,* February 1985.

132

133

134

135

136

137

138

City: Makkah, Kingdom
of Saudi Arabia
Client: King Abdul Aziz
University
Unbuilt project

*Despite the desire of Saudi Arabia
to reproduce American buildings,
we took a direction not only
related to the spatial and
architectural tradition of the Mid-
East, but also forced by the aridity
of the land, heat of the sun, and
unforgiving character of all other
aspects of the natural
environment. It was natural that
the master plan and design of the
buildings take on the quality of a
desert village, for survival in those
villages came through
experimentation over centuries. We
reproduced those experiments in
laboratories in forms and shapes
very similar to those of the past.
No attempt was made to create
traditions which never existed, but
similarity of forms arose out of
pragmatic considerations and
translation of those considerations
into an architectural vocabulary
responsive to the lifestyle and
psyche of desert dwellers.*

The 467-acre site for the university
is located in a valley surrounded by
low, barren mountains west of the
holy city of Makkah, in the Kingdom of Saudi Arabia. The Makkah-
Jeddah Road, which is the principal highway to Makkah for thousand's of annual Haj pilgrims, provides a natural separation of the
site into two distinct sections: one
for the academic complex, the other for dependent housing. The academic complex was intended to
reflect the social, cultural, and
historic pattern of Saudi Arabi-
an life, and was itself separated
into two campuses, one for men,
the other for women. Full enroll-
ment was expected to reach fifteen
thousand with an estimated ten
thousand men and five thousand
women.

139

The master plan for the University
reflects traditional Islamic urban
settlements. Like those commun-
ities, the campuses were to consist
of tightly clustered low-rise buildings; a vehicle-free, pedestrian-ori-
ented environment was a primary
objective. Buildings were designed
to respond to Makkah's extreme
climate and to maximize air ventilation and natural light.

Bibliography: Albenaa, 1982; *Architectural
Review,* January 1979; *Building News,* August 1979; *Middle East Construction,* October 1981; *Montgomery Journal,* 25 April
1979; *Progressive Architecture,* October
1982; U.S. Department of Commerce. *An
Evaluation of Thermal Energy Conservation
Schemes for an Experimental Masonry
Building,* NBS Building Science Series, no.
137.

140. Model of women's library
141. Plan of courtyard and pedestrian
areas around ceremonial mosque
142. Central library courtyard

140

141

142

King Abdul Aziz University

143. Rendering of preliminary plan for ceremonial mosque

144. Patterns for tile

145. Rendering of administrative courtyard
146. Rendering of academic courtyard
147. Rendering of student pavilion
148. Rendering of student housing

144

145

146

147

148

City: Chicago, Illinois
Client: Gerald D. Hines Interests,
Houston, Texas
Fifty-seven story office tower;
nine-story glass enclosed entry
lobby
Steel structure; granite cladding;
tinted glass

*As we began to master the tube
structures for tall buildings, we
gained the ability of setting up
rules and breaking them without
violating the structure, without
compromising integration. We
were in search of an expression
that would allow these
uncompromised structures to land
on earth gently and yet celebrate
the romance of towers. Three First
National was one of many such
adventures. The grid is preserved
but broken down so as to
articulate movement from street to
building.*

The fifty-seven story tower is located between the financial center and
downtown commercial district of
the Chicago Loop. The granite-clad
building is entered through a nine-
story glass-enclosed atrium and is
linked to the neighboring First
National Bank building by a second-level walkway. Rising above
the atrium, the tower's sawtoothed
setback design minimizes the dis-
ruption of views from nearby buildings, provides multiple corner offices, and affords tenants abundant
natural light and a variety of views.
This same configuration is accentu-
ated on the top six levels by stepped
greenhouses facing Lake Michigan.
The tower's tubular structural system provides strong wind resis-
tance and allows column-free interior spaces. Office areas and mezzanine balconies look onto the central
atrium. A stepped steel truss structure repeats the sawtooth geometry
on an inclined plane and supports
the clear glass enclosure. The atrium lobby provides protected pedestrian access to Chicago's underground arcade network and to the
city's rapid transit system.

Bibliography: Architecture and Urbanism,
March 1983; *Chicago Architectural Journal,*
1981; 1982; *Chicago Sun-Times,* 8 May
1983; *Proq. Arquitectura Diseno Urbanismo
Industrias,* April 1984; *Space Design,* May
1979.

149

150

151

152

153

154

City: Chicago, Illinois
Client: Miglin-Beitler Developments
Forty-five story office building
Structural steel tube; grey polished granite; silver reflective glass; polished stainless steel trim

Madison Plaza is another such tower, simpler, and yet more powerful. A raised triangular entry plaza, paved in a grid pattern, at the corner of the block, enhances the quality of the intersection. I can well imagine four such buildings at an intersection, creating a space that signifies the gateway or crossing, such as those found in Barcelona.
Unique office spaces are provided in this forty-five story office building. The glass front elevation is a sawtooth form which rises from the entrance plaza to the sloped roof of the thirty-ninth and forty-fourth floors. The steel tube structure is clad with bands of silver reflective glass and light gray polished granite. Window sizes vary to provide optimum views of the surrounding city and to respond to energy considerations. By setting the building back from the street, a triangular elevated entry plaza was formed to buffer the building entrance from the heavy street traffic and the adjacent elevated rapid transit tracks. The plaza also provides an appropriate setting for a sculpture by Louise Nevelson.
The lobby is finished in statuary Bettogi marble with polished stainless steel trim. Stainless steel elevator doors are etched with a subtle grid. The elevator interiors are mahogany paneled with a custom ceiling of stainless steel and luminous panels. Individual tenant floors provide a maximum of eight corner offices, all offering views to the central Loop business district and the lake beyond.
A structural steel system was chosen to respond efficiently to cost and construction requirements as well as to the unique architectural

155

98

157. Southeast facade showing saw-tooth profile and silver glass reflecting image of the Sears Tower

157. Southeast facade showing saw-tooth profile and silver glass reflecting image of the Sears Tower

configuration of the building. The structural steel superstructure has an exterior framed tube interacting with a full-height braced steel core. The framed tube system was developed using fifteen-foot-wide shop fabricated "tree" units which were welded and field bolted at the middle of the spandrel beam span. These tree units eliminated most of the field welding, industrialized the production of the tree units in the shop, and, therefore, resulted in a high erection speed of three to five floors per week.

Bibliography: Architecture and Urbanism, March 1983; Chicago Tribune, 3 May 1981; 22 July 1985.

158

159

158. Model showing unbuilt second phase
159. Exterior from the southeast

160. Plaza with Louise Nevelson sculpture
161. Exterior looking up through sculpture
162. Entrance lobby

161

160

162

**Grupo Industrial Alfa,
Corporate Headquarters**

City: Monterrey, Mexico
Client: Grupo Industrial Alfa
Concrete structure finished
in stucco

*Grupo Industrial Alfa in
Monterrey, Mexico was a response
to an entirely different situation.
The city is dynamic, but
struggling for survival in a
country that is exciting, but
fraught with its troubled identity.
The language so clearly set by
Luis Barrágan gives hope where
there should be none. Into that
language we incorporated what
was now my tradition—structural
viability. Mexico's climate, while
not as intense as Saudi Arabia,
approximates that lack of
hospitality, so public spaces were
enclosed in a gallery that became
the public room for employees.*

Situated at the foot of the Sierra
Madre Oriental Mountains on a
twenty-five-acre wooded site, the
Grupo Industrial Alfa headquarters facility was designed to take
advantage of the natural setting
and mountain views. The complex
includes executive offices, general
offices, a large auditorium and employee cafeteria all united by a
barrel-vaulted galleria. In keeping
with the traditions of Mexican
landscape design, the facility features planted courtyards, formal
open courts, and a large garden
court with trellis. Exterior sunshades, both horizontal and vertical, are found throughout the
building and are used for energy
control over the setback windows.
The punched windows are glazed in
clear glass and provide light pene-
tration into the building's interior
zones. The concrete structure is
finished in stucco.

163

164

163-165. *Views of model*
166, 167. *Elevations*
168. *Lower level and main level plans*

165

West

166

South

167

Lower Level

1. Entry Court
2. Semi Covered Parking
3. Ancillary
4. Service Mechanical Spine
5. Loading Dock
6. Hon. President's Parking
7. Limousine Plaza
8. Gen. Directors Parking
9. Mechanical

Main Level

1. Lobby Reception
2. Employee Cafeteria
   a. Kitchen
   b. Serving
   c. Dining
3. General Office Area
   a. Private Offices
   b. Ancillary
4. Sculpture Court
5. Directors Area
   a. Reception
   b. Ancillary
   c. Private Offices

Building Plans

1:250   April 1979

ASK 2

168

169. *Barrel-vaulted galleria*

169

170

**National Gallery Extension,
Design Competition**

171

City: London, England
Client: London Land Investment
and Property Company, Ltd.

*The National Gallery Extension
was my first major experience
with the weight of tradition that
began centuries before America's
discovery. The approach was that
of filling in a void. London is a
medieval city that has endured
intervention over the centuries
without the destruction of its
inherent character. The proposed
solution for the Gallery was, first
and foremost, one of respect for
the grand collection of art, and
therefore, an extension of the
grandness of these works into the
building design. We also proposed
to express the whole of the Gallery
in sympathy with the buildings of
Trafalgar Square. In order to do
so, our materials were Portland
Stone and bronze yet in a modern
vernacular that included both the
scale and texture of the
surrounding architecture. The
subtle moves of previous architects
had to be complemented, not
destroyed, in this national square
of London.*

The design for the new extension
respects the building line of the
existing facade while also recognizing the overall axial dynamics of
Trafalgar Square. The height, texture, and massing of the new extension are consistent with the
surrounding buildings and restate
their scale, while its facade, like
those of the neighboring Canada
House, the United University Club
building, and the National Gallery,
is clad with Portland stone and
articulated with granite and bronze
detailing.

On the interior, the new gallery is
formally linked to the existing gallery by means of an axial progression of interconnecting galleries
running east to west. A north-south

Rendered view of the Trafalgar Court looking north

Rendered view of the Gallery Entry Court

Rendered view of the St. Martin's Walk looking south to the St. Martin's Court

172

171. *Rendering of exterior*
172. *Plan and renderings of entrance*
173. *Plans of lower and ground floor levels; renderings of gallery shop and coffee shop; elevation and section of new gallery*
174. *Ground floor plan; elevation of National Gallery with new extension*

axis of galleries establishes the new gallery's own planning and architectural identity, allowing for set pieces, displays, and terminating vistas for principal and monumental works as well as more intimate spaces for smaller-scale works. The formal arrangement of spaces establishes a logical sequence of movement through the rooms of the new gallery to the major room fronting Trafalgar Square, allowing the visitor to the new gallery glimpses of the surrounding architectural environment.

The central rooms of the new gallery maintain the Renaissance theme of order, not only through their hierarchy of spaces and the progression of movement from gallery to gallery, but also through a careful choice and ordering of materials and design elements. The tone and texture of the materials used throughout remains elegant and uncluttered, so as to place the main visual emphasis on the works of art displayed. Thus, the walls and floors of the central rooms are of travertine marble, and the main flanking galleries feature plaster walls with a travertine marble base and polished oak floors bordered in travertine.

Bibliography: *Apollo*, January 1985; *Architect's Journal*, October 1982; *Architectural Review*, December 1982; *Chicago Tribune*, 14 December 1982; *Financial Times*, 24 August 1982; *Skyline*, November 1982; *The Standard*, 23 August 1982; 25 August 1982.

173

174

175

176

177

Huntington Center,
Office Building

City: Columbus, Ohio
Client: Gerald D. Hines Interests
Thirty-seven story office tower
Steel structure with granite
cladding

Huntington Center in Columbus, Ohio, was inspired by the existing State Capitol Building on the State House Lawn, which reaches out toward the Scioto River. Our goal was to split the tower in order to make a visual gateway, while at the same time create an entry and multi-storied atrium that would turn a box-like quality of office space into poetic spaces for those who spend more than half their waking hours in such buildings.

The thirty-seven story Huntington Center office tower is situated along an axial corridor that originates with the Ohio State Capitol building to the east and terminates at the Scioto River to the west. The glass and steel multi-atrium core is recessed from the red granite-clad office tower, creating an overall effect of two towers linked by glass. A symmetrical sawtooth plan provides sixteen corner offices on each floor. The top of the tower rises two stories in a series of stepped greenhouses to create penthouse office space. A nine-story lobby affords tenants and visitors an expansive view of the surrounding city. Covered walkways at the second level connect to the existing Huntington National Bank Building to the north and to the Center's attached low-rise hotel and parking structure to the west.

178

179

Bibliography: Capitol Magazine, 11 December 1983; *Corporate Design & Realty,* September 1986.

0 5 10   20

180

178. Construction photograph of the east facade
179. Detail of facade
180. Typical floor plan
181, 182. Exterior views

181

182

Josep Llorens Artigas
Foundation Studio

City: Gallifa, Spain
Client: Joan Gardy Artigas

The Artigas Foundation Studio in Gallifa, Spain is a direct interpretation of the natural materials available to builders in the surrounding mountains and also relates to an ancient chapel and mill on the site. Again, the search for technology does not necessarily mean that power should be used where it is not needed. It was indeed a labor of respect for those who worked here from Artigas to Miro to the younger Artigas.

Set into the sloped and terraced countryside of old vineyards and scattered woods north of Barcelona, the Spanish artist Joan Gardy Artigas commissioned a small complex of artist's studios dedicated to the memory of his father, the famed Catalonian ceramist Josep Llorens Artigas. Recognizing the atmosphere of excitement and insight provoked by international exchange and collaboration, the Josep Llorens Artigas Foundation Studio provides work space and living accommodations for visiting artists from around the world. The Studio includes facilities for work in ceramics, painting, printmaking, and sculpture and provides a commons area for study, conversation, and display.

Linked by a series of stone walkways and simply landscaped courtyards, the complex is composed of two-level buildings resting on separate terrace levels in a manner that complements both the Spanish village tradition and the local landscape. Masonry and concrete bearing walls articulated by wood windows support wood-framed, terra cotta tile roofs. Two structures are divided to create four two-level studios while a third houses four lower-level apartments and an upper-level commons area. The studios flank a communal Japanese stepped kiln.

The deliberately basic and restrained design is devoid of decoration, but provides an abundance of variable daylighting, natural ventilation, passive solar and fireplace heat, and outdoor spaces of varied character and function to create an environment that will encourage each visitor's artistic development. It is hoped that the compound will evolve with each artistic association, eventually becoming adorned with spontaneously placed tiles, murals, and sculptures. Adjacent to a medieval chapel and an ancient mill, the Foundation will take its place among sturdy, ageless structures whose character is shaped by the natural forces of the surrounding countryside.

Bibliography: Chicago Architectural Journal 5, 1985.

183

183. East-west section and lower level plan
184. Upper level
185. Site plan

184

185

186. Model
187. Site showing pre-existing buildings
188. Detail of artist's studio

186

187

188

City: Atlanta, Georgia
Client: Taylor and Mathis

Two two-phased twin atrium office buildings with terraced, landscaped parking garages

Structural concrete frame, paint coated; clear glass recessed window wall; suspended sunshading. Atria: natural wood windows and railings; glazed ceramic tile fountains and floors

The Terraces at Perimeter Center were an extension of the ideas found in the BMA building in Kansas City. Evocative of a huge Sol LeWitt sculpture, Perimeter Center is gently articulated within a large frame, a frame that captures space not only horizontally, but vertically. The structure is simple and is eroded where it is not required, thereby giving a sense of suspension when you are in fact suspended, and a sense of gravity when you are in fact on the ground. The integration now of more sophisticated environmental-engineering knowledge allowed for the elimination of tinted glass in a climate where that had become a tradition. Instead, we employed clear vision glass protected from direct sunlight by aluminum sun shades so that we were able to keep the views of that marvelous landscape and of the explosions of flowers that make up an endless Georgian tradition.

The Terraces at Perimeter Center are part of an office park development located on five hundred acres of gently rolling countryside north of Atlanta, Georgia. The two-phase project, consisting of twin atrium office buildings and two parking structures, has been carefully sited to complement the surrounding forest and to provide tenants with panoramic views. The wooded landscape of the site has been further enhanced by a series of ponds fed by an existing creek and spanned by a cable-supported pedestrian bridge.

Each ten-story building features two office wings connected at each level by bridges that span the central atria. Visitors enter the

189

ELEVATION

SECTION

buildings from square terraces paved in geometric patterns of red clay brick and gray granite. Copper-roofed wooden canopies provide shelter over the terraces from inclement weather. Deep exterior fountain ponds are continued inside each atrium where they are transformed into shallow pools formed of handmade, glazed ceramic tiles by the Barcelona ceramist Joan Gardy Artigas. These same colorful tiles have been combined with industrial quarry tiles to form rich and exuberant paving patterns in the atria and elevator lobbies. Each office building is composed of a poured-in-place concrete frame finished with a white architectural coating. The upper portion of the frame is stepped-back, creating a series of terraces from the seventh to the tenth floors. The buildings are glazed with clear-vision and insulated spandrel glass that is recessed from the facade and protected from the strong Georgian sunlight by aluminum solar fins. This articulation of the buildings' surfaces maximizes both energy efficiency and views of the surrounding landscape.

Bibliography: Architectural Record, July 1988; *Architecture & Technology*, no. 9, 1988; *The Atlantic Journal*, 29 October 1984; *The Chicago Architectural Journal*, 1983; *Inland Architect*, November/December 1988.

0 10 25 50   100   200 ft

191

The Terraces at Perimeter Center

*191, 192. Exterior views of the buildings
in landscape setting*
193. Peristyle and parking garage
*194. Exterior of north and south buildings
with connecting bridge*

192

193

194

195

195. Peristyle seen from office building
196. View through exposed structure
of building to path and gazebo
197. Elevator lobby with ceramic tiles
by Artigas
198. Exposed structure of exterior

196

197

198

199

200

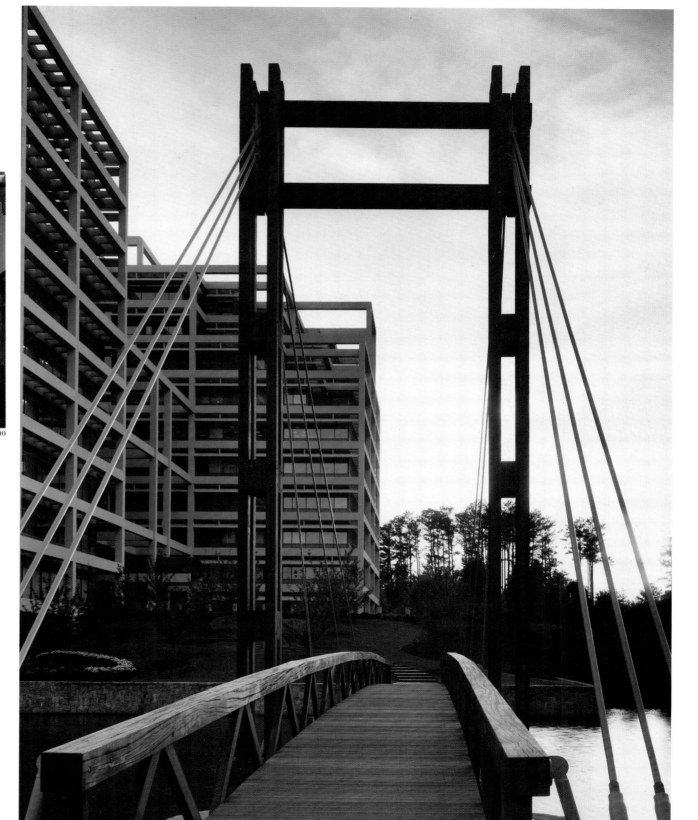

201

City: Chicago, Illinois
Clients: One Financial Place
Partnership, Chicago Exchange
Building Corporation
Three linked office buildings:
Chicago Board Options Exchange
(seven stories); One Financial
Place (thirty-nine stories);
Midwest Stock Exchange (six
stories); connected by a glass
bridge to the Chicago Board of
Trade Complex

*One Financial Place is a series of
buildings not designed as one, but
rather as a sequence of buildings
envisioned, prior to commission, as
an important piece of the city of
Chicago. It is intended to celebrate
the primary gate into the city, if
not in the way Daniel Burnham
conceived, certainly in a way
sympathetic to the idea. One
Financial Place operates within
the realization that buildings are
but pieces of cities. The need for*

*architects to collaborate in a
common vision and common
purpose is more apparent in
America than in the already
established cities of Europe.*
One Financial Place is the central
building of a complex comprising
the seven-story Chicago Board Options Exchange (CBOE) and the
six-story Midwest Stock Exchange.
The three-building complex is
linked physically and electronically
with the Chicago Board of Trade.

The thirty-nine story tower provides office space specially designed for the financial community
and adjoining exchanges, a health
club, restaurants, and a one-story
commercial building. The exterior
walls of the structural steel building
consist of a high performance curtain wall with Imperial Red granite
cladding and bronze-tinted vision
glass.
A block-long landscaped plaza, including a fountain and sculpture,

Chicago Board of Trade
Holabird & Root

Addition
Helmut Jahn

Chicago Board Options Exchange
SOM

One Financial Place
SOM

Midwest Stock Exchange
SOM

202

establishes the complex as a gateway to Chicago's south financial district. The granite-clad and paved plaza not only provides two entrances to the complex and underground parking, but also complements the Imperial Red granite used on each of the three structures.

Two covered exterior arcades and a ground level interior concourse link the three buildings, while the complex also provides connections to the subway, elevated and commuter lines. A bridge connects the entire complex to the Chicago Board of Trade, thereby creating the largest contiguous trading floor area in the United States, as well as providing exchange members with controlled interior circulation. The bridge itself is a steel truss structure fabricated as two units at the factory and assembled on-site. While the CBOE building was designed to accommodate the bridge without additional structural support, a large pier was necessary to support the bridge where it attaches to the Board of Trade addition.

Bibliography: *Chicago Sun-Times*, 28 April 1983; 18 July 1983; 20 December 1984; *Chicago Tribune*, 9 July 1982; 4 September 1984; 9 October 1984; 21 October 1984; 19 January 1986; 30 August 1987; *The Christian Science Monitor*, 19 April 1984.

203

One Financial Place

204

205

208

209

208, 209. *Exterior and interior view of glazed pedestrian bridge over Van Buren Street between the Chicago Board of Trade addition and the Chicago Board Options Exchange*

210. *Lobby of One Financial Place*

210

McCormick Place Exposition Center, Expansion Facility

City: Chicago, Illinois
Client: Metropolitan Fair and Exposition Authority
Twelve pylons on a 120×240 foot grid support the 480×780 foot cable suspended roof

The McCormick Place Exposition Center, Expansion Facility, is counterpart to the McCormick Place building by C.F. Murphy on Chicago's lakefront. The site is encumbered by active railroad tracks which prohibit casual placing of structural elements. In order to provide a long-span roof system, the simplest solution was to support the large roof by suspended cables which, in turn, are supported by concrete pylons. On the interior, these pylons not only provide support for the roof truss system, but are also equipped with air circulation systems.
For the expression of such a pavilion, and for the selection and

design of the exterior walls, we were certainly aware of Mies van der Rohe, but we were much more aware of the existing gigantic facility in black, so white became a natural color for what is, comparatively, a much lighter structure. Light gains entry into the building through roof skylights and through a perimeter band of glazing directly below the roof truss, lending the interior a museum-like quality, so that glare does not disturb the visitors.

The expansion of the McCormick Place Exposition Center Expansion Facility along Chicago's lakefront was prompted by both an increasing demand for space suffi-

cient in size to service large trade shows and the desirability of a convention/exhibition space capable of accommodating two major shows simultaneously. Enclosed pedestrian bridges connect the building to the adjacent exhibition facilities. In addition to the exhibition space consisting of upper level and lower level exhibit halls, the expansion facility provides meeting rooms, food service, enclosed crate storage and other ancillary services. The structural-steel, low-rise building utilizes a cable-supported roof system that allows long, clear spans and solves difficult site constraints related to the existing railroad which traverses the site. A

211

600 × 1,350 foot elevated podium spans the operating railroad lines while the building rises from that podium in two distinct parts: a fifty-five foot high main exhibition hall and a twenty-two foot high crate storage area. The 480 × 780 foot long-span roof over the main exhibition hall is suspended from cables supported by twelve concrete pylons projecting sixty feet above the roof level. Slender tiedowns at the exterior ends of the cable system restrain structural movement. The facade is clad with silver-gray aluminum panels framed by polished stainless steel mullions.

The 375,000 square foot upper level exhibition hall is based on the 120 × 240 foot grid of the twelve pylons. The lower level hall has a structural grid of 30 × 60 foot spans and measures approximately 150,000 square feet.

Bibliography: *Architecture*, March 1988; *Building Design & Construction*, January 1985; *Chicago Architectural Journal*, 1981; *Chicago Sun-Times*, 5 September 1984; 10 March 1985; *Chicago Tribune*, 18 November 1982; 8 March 1987; *Dodge Construction News*, 25 March 1985; *Inland Architect*, January-February 1985; *Progressive Architecture*, February 1989.

212

McCormick Place Exposition Center, Expansion Facility

213. *View from Lake Michigan*
214. *View from southeast*
215. *Entrance*
216. *Cable support system for roof*

213

214

215

216

**McCormick Place Exposition Center,
Expansion Facility**

217

218

219

220

McCormick Place Exposition Center, Expansion Facility

221. Interior of lower level exhibit hall showing Y columns which carry utility cables

221

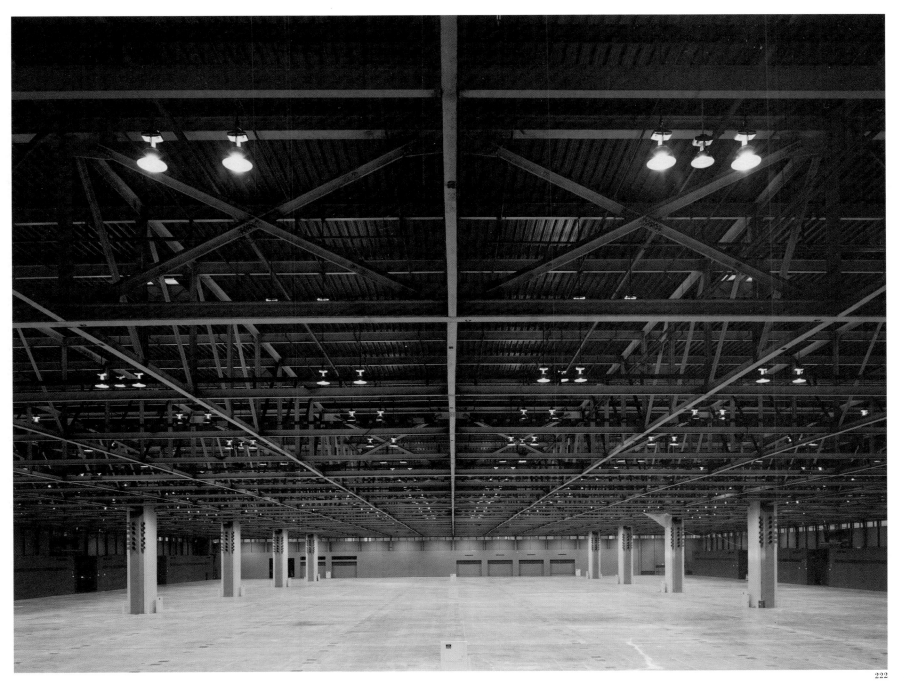

222

City: London, England
Client: Olympia and
York/Canary Wharf
Development Corporation

Three major plans underway in London have convinced me even more that collaboration between architects is possible, and that ego in either architecture or planning does not serve our cities well. So with architect Henry Cobb and landscape architect Laurie Olin at Canary Wharf, we searched diligently for rules with which to play this collaboration game. Now others, such as Cesar Pelli, Kohn Pederson Fox, and SOM's Adrian Smith, have entered into the design of individual buildings and have become aware of the need to collaborate not only with one another, but also with Nash, Soane, Wren, and Hawksmoor. There are reasons, both physical and psychological, for the shape and form of existing buildings: social structures have changed, the psyche and mentality of modern man is different, and certainly the technology with which we make buildings has changed. But, these changes can and should be subtle and sensitive to the overall composition of a great city.

Canary Wharf is on the Isle of Dogs in the Borough of Tower Hamlets, two miles east of the City of London. Formerly part of the Port of London, the site is under the aegis of the London Docklands Development Corporation, an agency established by the government to promote the regeneration of a vacated eight square mile area. Linked to the city by road, rail, and river, the proposed Canary Wharf development revitalizes seventy-one acres of the former West India Docks by providing ten million square feet of office space and financial trading floors, necessary to accommodate the expansion of London's crowded financial center, as well as its public recreational and retail facilities.

Throughout the design phase the original existing features of the site—the linear quay, the access roads and bridges, and the riverside—have remained of primary importance. The quay, built between 1800 and 1806 and once defined by the warehouses and an intricate system of locks vital to the

West India Company, will be transformed into a sequence of landscaped spaces. State of the art financial headquarters and commercial office buildings will be situated around the quay's outermost edges.

Placed beneath the quay will be a multi-level platform extending the full length of the wharf. The platform, acting as a service spine, will accommodate the utility distribution system, service roads, and car parks. Creation of this platform subtly elevates the public areas, and forms, in effect, a viewpoint from which to observe the River Thames.

The master plan includes three carefully located office towers. These landmark buildings, visible from the City, will enrich the London skyline and identify Canary Wharf from a distance. The remaining buildings will be of limited height, designed to frame and animate the sequence of landscaped areas that constitute the wharf's public realm. The full development of the site and the provision of open

223

space calls for buildings to be constructed over the water at points to the north and south of the wharf. Thus, the impounded water will no longer form a long linear passage, but a series of water courts ringed by pedestrian areas and linked by pedestrian promenades.

After a thorough study of London squares, parks, streets, and buildings, architectural guidelines were developed to ensure that each individual parcel would contribute to the image of the project as a whole. These guidelines include consistent use of cornice lines, stone bases, setbacks, street furniture, and other site elements both within and without the individual parcels. These elements, along with easements and riverside walkways, are intended to provide a continuous and varied pedestrian network.

224

Bibliography: Architect's Journal, 12 June 1985; *Architectural Review*, January 1986; *Architecture*, September 1988; January 1989; *Architecture & Technology*, no. 9, 1988; *Art and Design*, December 1985; *Building*, 27 September 1985; 25 October 1985; 13 December 1985; 24 January 1986; 25 September 1987; *Building Design*, 13 September 1985; 4 October 1985; 22 November 1985; 29 November 1985; 4 July 1986; 25 September 1987; *Euromoney*, October 1985; *London Daily Telegraph*, 25 May 1988; *New York Times*, 7 January 1986; 18 July 1987; *Progressive Architecture*, January 1989; *The Sunday Times*, 10 April 1988; *Time*, 18 April 1988; *Wall Street Journal*, 13 July 1987; 26 July 1988.

225

226

227

228

229

230

**Bishopsgate Project, Broadgate
Phases Five through Fourteen,
Multi-Use Complex**

City: London, England
Client: Rosehaugh Stanhope
Developments PLC

*So it was with Bishopsgate that
the client, Rosehaugh Stanhope
Developments, and authorities of
London were not only responsive,
but helpful in searching for the
solutions to goals while also
maintaining the rules of structure
and of spatial definition. We were
able, then, to manipulate those
rules so as to continue the very
useful definition of cities within
cities that makes up the grand city
of London. Where problem areas
once existed, we created spatial
relationships that established
urban opportunities.*

The Broadgate development is located in the northeastern portion
of the city of London. Essentially
an air-rights development, nearly
all of its approximately twelve
acres span the existing British Rail
platforms and the railway tracks of
Liverpool Street Station. The multi-use development expands the financial district of London by sup-
plying new office space and trading
floors and also enhances the surrounding transportation center and
urban district with new retail space
and parking facilities.

Phases six, seven, and eight form

the three-building ensemble fronting the Bishopsgate thoroughfare.
This complex establishes an identity both for the individual buildings
and for the entire development.
The three-building composition
consists of an eight-story structure
with three five-story towers linked
by two two-story conservatories.
The building entrances occur on
axis with each of the three towers.
The whole ensemble is tied together
at the bottom by a two-story light
colored stone clad base which encloses a pedestrian arcade. Above
this, a highly articulated facade is

231

composed of polished granite and glass panels. A metal window wall system is employed to express and reinforce the structural integrity of a panelized wall system, recalling the texture and detail of traditional stone and cast-iron building. The entire facade is unified by elegantly detailed cornices at the second, fourth, eighth and twelfth floors. While the design of the Bishopsgate exterior is meant to recall the architectural order of grand compositions found throughout London, the interior speaks to its modern program through the use of elegant materials and functional design. Pedestrians using the main entrance from the east side of Bishopsgate are greeted by an arcade of select shops before entering the building lobbies. At the south end of the complex, commuters from Liverpool Street Station conveniently have access to the buildings through a pedestrian walkway running along the west side of the building complex. Levels one through three are trading floors while office space occupies floors four through twelve. Diffused light is admitted to the interior of the office space by skylit atria extending from floors four through nine. The design strategy for the Phase eleven building was to span the British Rail train tracks in the manner of a bridge. After studying a number of appropriate structural options, a parabolic arch was determined to be the most efficient solution. This singular structural concept was then expanded to create a functional and elegant architectural solution for the project, recalling the tradition of steel and glass structures built in Britain at the turn of the century.

The four parallel arches which support Phase eleven, along with the disposition of the various service elements, provide the architectonic strength of the project. The structure allows for large, column-free office and trading floor areas, with fire stairs, firemen's elevators, modular toilet room units, and plant rooms located in twin service towers which are clearly expressed as ancillary structures. The lobby and elevator shafts are hung from the building structure which allows for the movement differential between the lobby and the plaza. The lobby is enclosed with clear glass so as to appear nonstructural, and the elevator enclosures and cabs are also glazed to enhance the transparency of the lobby. The structural expression is carried inside to the office floors by the twin atria, which are set between the inner arches, flanking the elevators and mechanical core. The atria are staggered in section, in recognition of the vault of the arches. Vision glass is fire-rated, allowing the exterior steel structure to be exposed, further enhancing the purity and clarity of the tectonic expression.

Bibliography: Architects' Journal, February 1988; December 1988; *Architecture,* February 1989; *Architecture & Technology,* no. 9, 1988; *Building Design,* 4 March 1988; *Chicago Architectural Journal,* vol. 6, 1987; *London Daily Telegraph,* 25 May 1988; *Progressive Architecture,* January 1989; *Wall Street Journal,* 26 July 1988.
The Chicago Tapes, introduction by Stanley Tigerman, Rizzoli, New York 1987.

232

233

Phase 2

3 Finsbury
Avenue

Finsbury
Avenue
Square

Phase 1

Sun Street

Central Square

Phase 3

Phase 5

Appold Street

Phase 4

Pindar Street

Phase 9/Phase 10

BRITISH RAIL
SIGNAL BOX SITE

WESTERN TRAINSHED

Phase 11

Primrose Street

Worship Street

Phase 12/Phase 13

GREAT
EASTERN HOTEL

Phase 6

Phase 7

Phase 8

Phase 14

Norton Folgate

Bishopsgate

234

236. *Rendering of east elevation,*
Phases 6, 7, 8

237, 238. *Model of east elevation*

East Elevation   This Area Shown For Illustrative Purposes Only

236

237

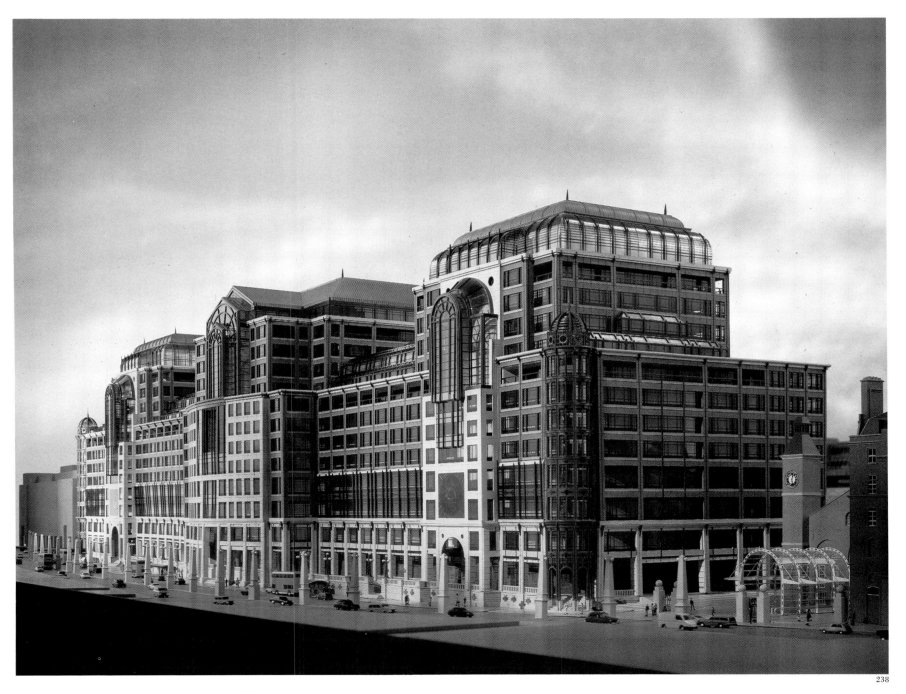

238

Bishopsgate Project, Broadgate

239. *Exterior detail of Phases 9-10*
240. *Exterior detail of Phases 6-7*
241. *Exterior detail of Phases 9-10*

242. *Exterior detail of Phase 5*
243. *Exterior detail of Phase 6*

239

240

241

242

243

244

244, 245. Interior pedestrian arcade linking Phases 6, 7, 8 from Liverpool Street Station to Exchange Square

245

246

247

248

249

250

251

252

253

254

250. Detail of model, Phase 11
251-254. Details of Phase 11 under
construction

255, 256. Computer-generated studies
of stairway, Phase 11

257. Phase 11 under construction

255

256

257

1987-1988   **King's Cross, Master Plan**   *258. Site plan*
*259. Rendering of master plan showing
St. Pancras Station on left and King's
Cross Station on right*

Associate Architects: Frank O.
Gehry & Associates; Hanna-Olin,
Inc.; Tigerman Fugman &
McCurry; Chipperfield Associates
City: London, England
Client: London Regeneration
Consortium PLC

*It has become even more apparent
at King's Cross through
collaboration with Frank Gehry,
Stanley Tigerman, Laurie Olin,
David Chipperfield, and other
consultants, that Camden is a
town with a soul, with citizens
who have pride and hope, and that
a plan for this large missing piece
can help fulfill the hopes and
aspirations of that society.
Fortunately, the clients feel the
search is worthwhile and that an
answer is possible. Here, we are
not just searching for building
forms and shapes, but for a
definition of the kinds of space
between buildings that give a
sense of reality to the buildings.
These spaces will not be the same
as those of the last century. Elitist
society does not play as
commanding a role as it did then;
it now has to learn to serve. We
are no longer interested in simply
designing objects, but in fulfilling
the role of architecture in the
design of cities.*

The King's Cross Master Plan was
a response to the request from the
London Borough of Camden and
British Rail for redevelopment of
the rail properties north of the
King's Cross and St. Pancras stations. The Plan was meant as a
reconfiguration and improvement
of the rail operations of the two
landmark stations.
Covering approximately 120 acres,
the King's Cross site is located in
the northern fringe of Central London near the West End and the
City. The layout of the Master Plan
is generated by the orientation of
the two landmark stations of King's
Cross and St. Pancras and the
respective alignment of their railway tracks. The street grid and
orientation of buildings in the western section follow the alignment of
St. Pancras, while those of the
eastern section follow the alignment of King's Cross. The basic
planning diagram consists of two
major gateways into the development, one at the southern frontage

between the two stations and the
other on York Way to the northeast of the extended Regent's Canal, which flows through the site.
The Master Plan divides the site
into five sectors. The southern sector or "King's Place" is intended
to be a prestigious new office center
with support retail close to the
enhanced railway facilities. The
central sector called "Battlebridge
Island" is to be a mixed-use area
that incorporates a hotel, heritage
center, retail, leisure space, housing
and offices. "York Way" is the
eastern sector and features flexible
industrial/workshop facilities, offices and retail. Housing, community facilities, and open space constitute the "Camden Fields" northern
sector, and the "Camley Gardens"
western sector incorporates the enlarged Nature Park, St. Pancras
Gardens and a new entertainment
and leisure park along the Canal.

Bibliography: London Daily Telegraph, 25
May 1988; *Progressive Architecture,* January
1989.

258

Port Imperial, Master Plan and Multi-Use Development

Associate Architects: Venturi, Rauch, Scott Brown, Frank O. Gehry and Associates, Inc., Studio di architettura Aldo Rossi (Morris Adjmi), Charles Moore Studio
City: West New York, New Jersey
Client: Arcorp Properties

The hope of collaborating with others in an attempt to search for the language of cities has not only been my personal objective since early youth, but is also an objective of SOM. The pleasure of working with other architects and sharing visions of what might be must, in fact, be rewarding to any architect. In New Jersey, across from Manhattan, the recent charette with Frank Gehry, Charlie Moore, Steve Izenour, and David Childs proved my point. The speed with which our thoughts and ideas became architectural realities was as I expected. No man can build an entire city alone, perhaps no group of architects can build a city alone, but such groups can certainly project visions generated by our interpretations of the human spirit—that is what it's all about. It is this enjoyment of collaboration that drives SOM.

Directly across the Hudson River from Manhattan, the Port Imperial Multi-Use Development covers 125 acres of abandoned railroad yards. The development will be situated along the river at the foot of the Palisades to provide some seven-thousand housing units in three primary neighborhoods and 1,7 million square feet of commercial space concentrated around a crescent-shaped town center. The layout and massing of the development takes advantage of expansive views and maximizes the water-front amenities. An open space network with landscaping unites residential and commercial uses and brings the Palisades across the site in two major parks.
Development of the site will occur in stages throughout the 1990s.

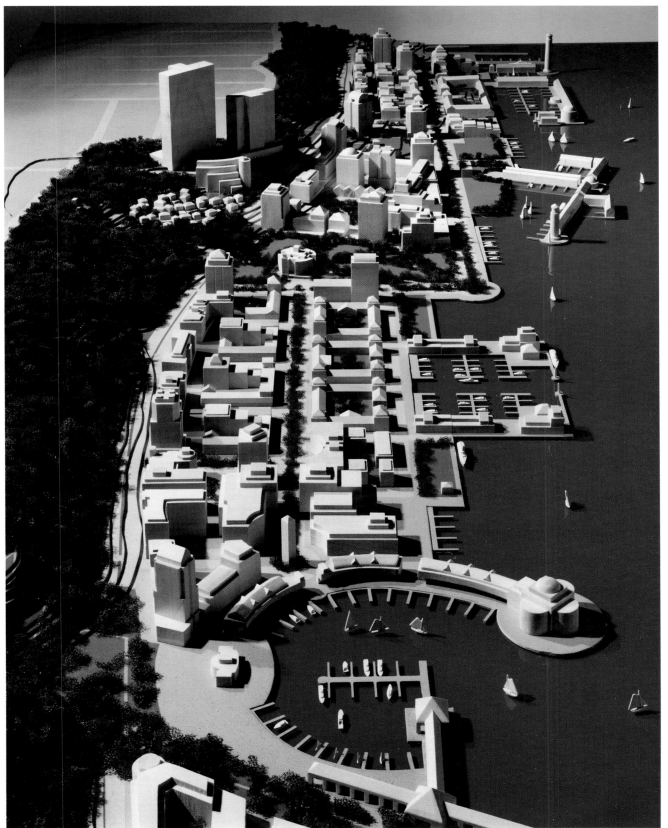

260. Aerial view of model

260

City: Uxbridge, England
Client: Stockley Park Consortium Ltd.
Three three-story office buildings; two of 119,000 square feet; one of 80,000 square feet; on-grade parking; landscaping
White painted aluminum, clear and fritted glass, pre-cast concrete, exposed steel roof frame

Office buildings in a park are the industrial buildings of our era. They become the ultimate flexible spaces; highly technological, but in the end a horror for workers who spend from eight to twelve hours in their confines. The new worker demands a more amenable environment. Material of concrete, steel and glass are assembled with a by-component of green nature so as to soften the tediousness of every day life. These buildings constitute the first one hundred percent computerized product at

SOM in that all drawings (architectural, structural and mechanical), are the product of a total design program which incidentally produces the construction documents.
Stockley Park is a 343-acre site situated near Heathrow, the major airport for London, England. The master plan for the site, a former landfill area, was developed in 1984 by Arup Associates to include a golf course by Robert Trent Jones and an extensively landscaped office park with buildings by Arup, Nor-

man Foster, SOM and others. The three buildings by SOM, slated for completion in 1990, are on an uneven triangular site bordered by a raised highway to the east and a canal on the south. A major concern of the client was the rooftop view of the buildings from the higher elevation of the golf course and highway. Thus the design solution for the three buildings incorporates a striking sculptural treatment of each roof. Another consideration in planning the site was the necessity of providing over 900

261

262

parking spaces. In response, a system of bays, partially concealed by berming and planting, was devised. A number of structural and mechanical options were explored through three-dimensional computer analyses to produce the most efficient and economical solution. The resulting 9-meter-square bay, used throughout, was logically expressed in the square plan for two of the buildings. The third building, while incorporating the same bay size, is irregular in plan in response to the site. The base of each building, is finished in pre-cast concrete. A white painted aluminum curtain wall, glazed with a combination of clear and fritted glass, is used for the two upper floors. The wall is stepped back at the top floor to expose the steel columns and give emphasis to the roof structure.

263

Stockley Park, Business Park Campus   *Computer-generated studies:*   *265. Entrance stair and canopy*   *266. Partial elevation of Building 9*
264. Meeting point of steel frame
and precast concrete

264

265

City: Chicago, Illinois
Client: Archdiocese of Chicago
Single-story 10,000 square feet
parish church with pitched roof
sanctuary, baptistry and Daily
Chapel with bell tower; 9,500
square feet multipurpose room
below grade; walled garden;
paved forecourt and entry plaza
White stucco over concrete and
concrete block with clear glass
set in black painted wood frames

*Holy Angels is an ancient problem
of man's search for God and one
which architects fear. For faith
was measured differently in the
late 19th century than in the late
20th century. But, the meeting
place for common prayer in a
community church, amidst the hell
of an American slum, is indeed a
primary responsibility and
opportunity. Simple materials
which can be understood by the
community, yet are formed in
traditions with echoes of the past,
will hopefully serve for the future.*

In 1986 the late 19th century Holy
Angels Parish Church burned to
the ground. The church had been
a lone symbol of hope in one of the
most depressed and violent neighborhoods in the United States.
Plans for the new church were
begun in 1989 with an overriding
concern in the design for simplicity,
flexibility and energy efficiency.
The basic basilica shape of the new
church is anchored at the northeast
by the chapel tower, marking the
Daily Chapel, and at the west end
by the glazed roof over the Baptis-

try. The main body of the church
is marked by a simple rhythm of
steel roof trusses, reaching a cele-
bration of light above the altar,
streaming down from dormer windows. The design also allows for
services to be said in the more
intimate space of the Daily Chapel,
still using the main altar which
rotates on a stone platform. The
pitched roof will carry solar panels
down the length of the south side,
which will provide most of the heat
for the church, backed up by a
traditional heating and cooling sys-

267

tem. The south wall of the church will also respond to the sun with a series of doors, glazed with clear glass, which can be thrown open to a walled garden beyond. By contrast the north wall, which faces the street, will be open only on the west end for the main entrance to the church, and for fourteen small wall openings containing dioramas by local artists depicting the Stations of the Cross. A plaza on the north and west sides of the church will be terraced concrete with stone paving, connecting the church to the parochial school of Holy Angels which will use the plaza for their playground. As cost efficiency was of paramount importance, the building has been designed to use standard components wherever possible. At the lower level there will be a multipurpose room running the whole length of the church with kitchen and support functions which can be adapted to many uses for the parish, community and school. The church will be connected to the adjacent rectory by a private access bridge.

268

269

163

Bruce Graham, design partner of SOM

Bruce Graham was born in La Cumbre, Bogota, Colombia in 1925, and completed his secondary education in South America. After two years in the U.S. Navy from 1943-1945, he graduated with a Bachelor of Architecture degree at the University of Pennsylvania in 1948. Since joining the firm in 1949, Mr. Graham has brought innovative aesthetic solutions to the varied requirements of major corporations, institutions and developers, not only in Chicago and across the United States, but also throughout the world in Hong Kong, England, Egypt, Spain and the Middle East. He was named a partner in charge of design in 1960. In the civic and professional realm, Mr. Graham's affiliations include the status of past president and current member of the Board of Directors for the Chicago Central Area Committee, a civic group of Chicago's most prominent business leaders, organized to direct the growth and development of Chicago's central area; a trustee of the Urban Land Institute and member of the Board of Directors of the Urban Land Research Foundation; member of the Commercial Club; Board member of the Chicago Council on Foreign Relations; honorary trustee of the Institute of Urbanism and Planning of Peru; Fellow of the American Institute of Architects, and a member of both the Royal Architectural Institute of Canada and the Royal Institute of British Architects. Mr. Graham is also active in the fields of education and the arts. In this capacity he serves as a trustee and chairman of the Board of Overseers for the School of Fine Arts at the University of Pennsylvania, a board mem-

ber of the Temple Hoyne Buell Center for American Architecture at Columbia University, a trustee of the Chicago Museum of Contemporary Art and of the Art Institute of Chicago, and a trustee of WTTW Channel 11.

Mr. Graham is the recipient of numerous awards. From the Royal Institute of British Architects he has received awards for the W.D. & H.O. Wills Corporate Headquarters and Tobacco Processing Company in Bristol, England, and Boots Pure Drug Company Ltd. Corporate Headquarters in Nottingham, England. He has received Honor Awards from the American Institute of Architects for the Business Men's Assurance Company of America in Kansas City, Missouri, and for the Banco di Occidente in Guatemala City, Guatemala. He has been honored with many awards from the Chicago Chapter of the American Insitute of Architects, including an Honor Award for the Inland Steel Building which in addition was designated an official landmark by the Commission on Chicago Architectural Landmarks, and Distinguished Building Awards for Baxter Travenol Laboratories, Inc., the John Hancock Center, the Sears Tower and the Chicago Board of Options Exchange Bridge. The Chicago Central Area Plan which was coordinated by Mr. Graham was awarded the Urban Design and Planning Award by Progressive Architecture.

Bibliographical Note

Fazlur R. Khan and Bruce Graham with model of the John Hancock Center

Articles by Bruce Graham

B.J. Graham, "The Search for a Postmodern Architecture." *The Architectural Student Journal*, Fall 1978.

B.J. Graham, "Architecture, Fashion and Advertising." *Inland Architect*, July 1978.

B.J. Graham, "The Architecture of Skidmore, Owings & Merrill." *Royal Institute of British Architects, Transactions* 2, no. 2 (1983): 76-84.

Articles and photographic features that include the work of Bruce Graham and SOM

Abitare, August 1987.
Architect's Journal, 25 May 1983; 16 September 1987.
Architectural Record, October 1972; March 1981.
Architecture, February 1989.
Arquitecto Peruano, March - June 1977.
Bauen & Wohnen, April 1957.
Building, August 1982; Oct. 1986.
Building Design, September 1973.
Building Design & Construction, August 1981.
Chicago, May 1982.
Chicago Sun-Times, 24 September 1985; 30 September 1985; 11 November 1985; 2 November 1986.
Chicago Tribune, 14 December 1980; 16 April 1981; 6 September 1981; 17 October 1982; 26 June 1983; 3 January 1984; 1 April 1985; 14 June 1985.
Harvard Graduate School of Design News, January/February 1987.
Inland Architect, July 1968; March/April 1984; March/April 1987.
Interiors, February 1975.
Newsweek, 8 November 1982.
Progressive Architecture, May 1981.
Proq. Architectura Piseno Urbanismo Industrias, April 1984.
Real Estate Advertiser, June 1983.

Books containing information on Bruce Graham, Bruce Graham's works and SOM

Art Institute of Chicago, *Chicago Architects Design, A Century of Architectural Drawings from the Art Institute of of Chicago*, Rizzoli, Chicago 1982.

I.J. Bach, ed., *Chicago's Famous Buildings*, The University of Chicago Press, Chicago 1980.

L. Benevolo, *L'ultimo capitolo dell'architettura moderna*, Editori Laterza, 1985.

A. Bush-Brown, *Skidmore, Owings & Merrill Architecture and Urbanism 1973-1983*, Verlag Gerd Hatje, Stuttgart 1983.

F. Chermayeff, *Observations on American Architecture*, The Viking Press, New York 1972.

S.E. Cohen, *Chicago Architects*, Swallow Press Inc., Chicago 1976.

C.W. Condit, *Chicago 1930-70*, The University of Chicago Press, Chicago 1974.

F. Dal Co and M. Tafuri, *Modern Architecture*, Harry N. Abrams, Inc., New York 1979.

E. Danz, *Architektur von Skidmore, Owings & Merrill, 1950-1962*, Verlag Gerd Hatje, Stuttgart 1962.

E. Danz, *Architecture of Skidmore, Owings & Merrill, 1950-1962*, Frederick A. Praeger, Publishers, New York 1963.

E. Danz and A. Menges, *La Arquitectura de Skidmore, Owings & Merrill, 1950-1973*, Editoriale Gustavo Gili, Barcelona 1975.

B. Diamonstein, *American Architecture Now II*, Rizzoli, N.Y. 1985.

A. Drexler, *Transformations in Modern Architecture*, Museum of Modern Art, New York 1979.

M. Emanuel, ed., *Contemporary Architects*, St. Martin's Press, New York 1980.

P. Guedes, *Encyclopedia of Architectural Technology*, McGraw-Hill Book Company, New York 1979.

P. Heyer, *Architects on Architecture*, Walker and Company, New York 1966.

A.L. Huxtable, *Kicked a Building Lately?*, Quadrangle/New York Times Book Co., New York 1976.

A.L. Huxtable, *The Tall Building Artistically Reconsidered*, Pantheon Books, New York 1984.

C. Jencks, *Skyscrapers - Skycities*, Rizzoli, New York 1980.

Macmillan Encyclopedia of Architects, The Free Press, N.Y. 1982.

A. Menges, *Architecture of Skidmore, Owings & Merrill, 1963-1973*, Architectural Book Publishing Co., New York 1974.

A.L. Morgan and C. Naylor, eds., *Contemporary Architects*, St. James Press, 2nd ed., Chicago 1987.

N.A. Owings, *The Spaces in Between: An Architect's Journey*, Houghton Mifflin Company, Boston 1973.

V. Scully, *American Architecture and Urbanism*, Holt Rinehart and Winston, New York 1969.

D. Sharp, *A Visual History of Twentieth-Century Architecture*, New York Graphic Society, Ltd., Greenwich 1972.

G.E.K. Smith, *The Architecture of the United States*, Anchor Press/Doubleday, Garden City 1981.

M. Whiffen and F. Koeper, *American Architecture 1607-1976*, The MIT Press, Cambridge 1981.

Who's Who In America, 4 vols., Macmillan Directory Division, Wilmette 1974-1981.

Who's Who in America, 1 vol., Macmillan Directory Division, Wilmette 1986-1987.

Photographic Credits

The numbers refer to the pages

©Altman, Ben, Sadin Photo Group, Chicago: 132, 134 (right), 135 (bottom), 136, 137, 150, 152 (left), 163

Cabanban, Orlando, Chicago: 58 (bottom), 102, 103, 109, 140 (left), 149

Carlos Diniz Associates, Los Angeles (Renderings): 92, 93, 139 (top), 140 (right), 141, 155

Fine, Robert, Chicago: 60 (top)

Hedrich-Blessing, Chicago: 10 (right), 11, 29 (bottom), 30, 31, 36 (top), 40, 46, 49 (left), 57, 58 (top), 76, 82 (top), 95, 96 (left), 97 (left), 100 (left), 101 (left), 101 (top), 108, 110 (top right), 111, 125, 126, 127, 128, 129, 133, 134 (left), 135 (top), 138, 146, 147

Hoyt, Wolfgang, ©Esto, Mamaroneck, N.Y.: 96 (right), 97 (right)

Hursley, Timothy, Little Rock: 47, 59, 60 (bottom), 61 (bottom), 116, 118, 119, 120, 121, 122, 123

Kaplan, Howard N., HNK Architectural Photography, Inc., Highland Park: 12, 13, 17 (right), 77 (top), 78 (bottom), 79, 81 (bottom), 91

Karant & Associates, Chicago: 82 (left)

Merrick Nick, Hedrich-Blessing, Chicago: 145, 147

Murphey, Gregory, Chicago: 98, 99, 100 (right), 101 (bottom)

Schmid, Robert: 114 (bottom)

Stoller, Ezra, ©Esto, Mamaroneck, N.Y.: 14, 15, 16, 17 (left), 18, 19, 22, 23, 24, 25, 26, 27, 29 (top), 32, 33, 34, 35, 39, 41, 43, 44, 45, 48, 49 (right), 50, 51, 52, 54, 56, 63, 64, 65, 66, 67, 68, 69, 70, 71, 72, 73 (bottom), 74, 75, 78 (top), 80, 81 (top), 82 (bottom), 83

Steinkamp-Ballogg Photography Chicago, Chicago: 157

Turner, Philip, Chicago: 38

Williams, Alan, London: 151, 152 (top left-right), 152 (bottom left-right), 153

Wheeler, Nick/Wheeler Photographics, Weston (Mass.): 84, 86, 87, 88, 89

DATE DUE

APR 1 6 2009			

HIGHSMITH 45230